CAMARO

CAMARO

RICHARD CARLYON

cp

This edition published in 1990 by
Chevprime Limited
an imprint of Brian Trodd Publishing House Limited
27 Swinton Street, London WC1X 9NW

ISBN 1 85361 110 7

Printed in Portugal

Additional editorial material supplied by John McGovren

Early testing for the 1985 Camaro IROC engine

CONTENTS

THE GUESSING GAME

A concept drawing produced in 1984, showing a fastback roofline.

Everyone at General Motors knew what was going on. Everyone that is except those who had it in their power to do something about it.

The designers knew, the modelers knew, the artists knew, the engineering staff knew, the concept planners knew, the admen knew, the PR men knew, the test-bed operators knew, the janitors knew. The top brass didn't know. Or if they did they showed no signs of it. The accountants didn't know, they believed their balance sheets.

Most of all, the public knew. Ford, GM's hottest rival, had scored a strike and were hotfooting it to home base with the help of their cheeky, sporty, runaway best-seller, the Mustang.

Over at Chevrolet they didn't believe that the Mustang was worth a row of beans, but the row of beans it wasn't worth turned out be sales of the Mustang to the tune of 400,000 plus in its first year.

Eventually the men in gray were convinced and set out to tame the wild pony. Suddenly everyone was working to bring out a Chevy that would compete with the Mustang. The brief was quite straightforward, the new car must compete with what had been produced by "those devils at Ford" (quote from Irv Rybicki, Chevy chief designer). That meant it had to have better styling, better looks inside and out, better engineering, more driver-response, tighter control, better acceleration and power, more speed and better suspension. It had to be wider, longer, lower and have more leg room; it had to be built at a competitive price that would still show a profit, and all this had to be done fast. Fast enough to catch up with the Mustang that was accelerating away down that turnpike signposted "sales."

The overall message was that GM were unhappy with being left in the weeds while Mustang Mania reigned supreme. This was August 1964. The Chevy-built Mustang-murderer had to be ready to burn rubber come the fall of 1966.

Where did they start? The answer is a little before the beginning. There had already been men at GM's drawing boards dreaming of a small, sporty, European-style car. The massive influx of British, German, and Italian cars in the 1950s had not gone unnoticed by the design and engineering professionals, and a few cars had begun the race against the foreign imports. Best-liked of these was Chevy's own Corvair and its follow-up, the Corvair Monza. In fact there is a good deal of truth in the statement that it was the Chevy Corvair Monza that motivated the redoubtable Lee Iacocca of Ford to push through his Mustang. Now Chevy had to answer back. They had already had a chance to get out a small car before Iacocca's Mustang, but it had been given shelf space by management instead of factory space. It had been a Rybicki idea supported and encouraged by Bill Mitchell, then GM styling VP. They got the idea to a clay model, proudly showed it to Bunkie Knudsen, Chevrolet general manager, only to be told "... the one thing we don't need right now is another car." End of story. The sting in the tail was that the proportions of this clay model were pretty nearly the same as the Mustang.

Then there was the attempt in 1964. This one was called the "Super Nova" and it was an "idea" car, a car designed to test out public reaction and to tease the opposition a little. This time Knudsen was eager, but his boss, Jack Gordon, said no. It took

Above: *Irv Rybicki, the chief designer at Chevrolet.*
Right: *S E (Bunkie) Knudsen, the general manager.*
Facing page: *Views of the 1964 Super Nova show car.*

This page: *Views of a refined earlier design.*
Facing page, top: *Hank Haga, who headed the Camaro design team.*
Center and bottom: *Design experiments with an RS front and a performance version.*

the rocketing Mustang sales to make GM management begin demanding what they had before rejected. According to Knudsen, GM management "were shocked to pieces when they found out how many had been sold."

Both Chevrolet and Pontiac were set to work designing the GM answer. Pontiac dipped in and out, for it had already gone some way to creating the shape of the famous Firebird-Trans Am.

At Chevrolet Hank Haga's design team responded enthusiastically to the challenge. They were all of them auto nuts and the idea of making the car to challenge Mustang was a dream come true for many of them.

They began with the Corvair, or at least with the philosophy behind the Corvair—the scraped-clean look of canvas tightly stretched over a simple wire frame. The shape was sharp at the nose with a strong rise to the prominent front wheel arch, a horizontal pulled-back feel to the second prominence, the rear wheel arch, and then a flow-off to a blunt, but still taut, rear end. The horizontal Coca Cola bottle feel. Unlike the Mustang the design they were after was not a scaled-down big car but a fresh, Italian-inspired shape. They sought purity of line and achieved it by putting aside any superfluous detail.

One extraordinary feature, eyecatching in its simplicity, was the enclosed front end; two horizontals joined with end curves, an egg-box grille and, look Mom, no lights. No lights! The impact of the RS variant with *hidden* headlamps is as startling today as it was then.

There was one more exterior detail that indicated the inspiration of many auto designers of the time. The machines that had made the deepest impression on designers' minds were the fighter planes of World War II. Echoes of these nearly mythical machines were to be heard in the names Mustang, Thunderbird and so on. The decoration, often stemming from practicality, was also caught and re-echoed. In the case of the Camaro it was the bumblebee stripe around the nose.

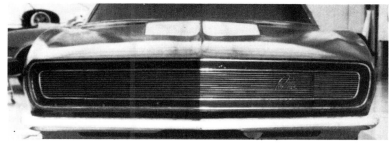

The designers had been looking at the way the area in front of fighter planes' cockpits had been painted matt black, to reduce reflection off the surface, they had also noticed the stripes around fighterplane air intakes; this was the cue for the nose stripe on the Camaro. In their opinion it gave the car a fighting, purposeful look and emphasized the lightless grille and provided definition for that unusual and good-looking nose.

The driver's interface with the machine is one of the most delicate areas to design, a good-looking set of instruments that are easy to read and create restful responsiveness will do much to persuade the customer to buy. After all, this will be his or her special place for a while to come, and if the environment says the right things the driver will feel proud to be seen in it.

George Angersbach, responsible for the interior design instrumentation of the Camaro, got into the mood by having a four-speed manual gear shift built onto his office chair. You could call him the inventor of the Method school of instrumentation design. It certainly produced results with a triple-pod look reminiscent of jetplane air-intakes, with a floor-mounted console extending back nearly to the rear seating area. The sloping center panel gave good hand access and the whole result proclaimed speed and precision. It also went some way towards satisfying the latent fighter plane ace fantasy that exists in a surprising number of drivers. How desirable this is we cannot say, but we have to admit that such fantasy does exist. Regrettably, Angersbach's console was adapted, but it still had tremendous flair.

Angersbach put together a precise interior that looked good, was functional, and which made the driver feel good. What all designers have to battle against all the time is not just the engineering feasibility of their work, but the cost as well. Not only do they have to design beautiful, they have to design possible as well. The Camaro interior designers did just that.

Above: *George Angersbach was in charge of the interior design instrumentation.*
Below: *The design at an advanced stage.*
Facing page: *Views of the instrument panel design in the early stages.*

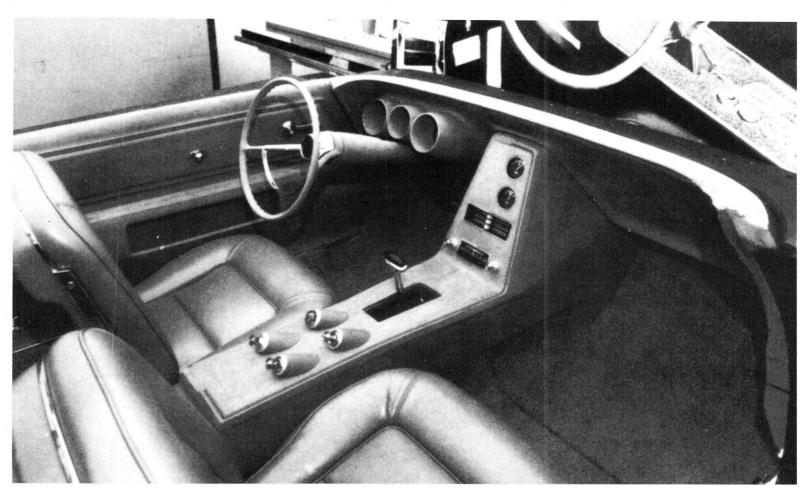

CLUES

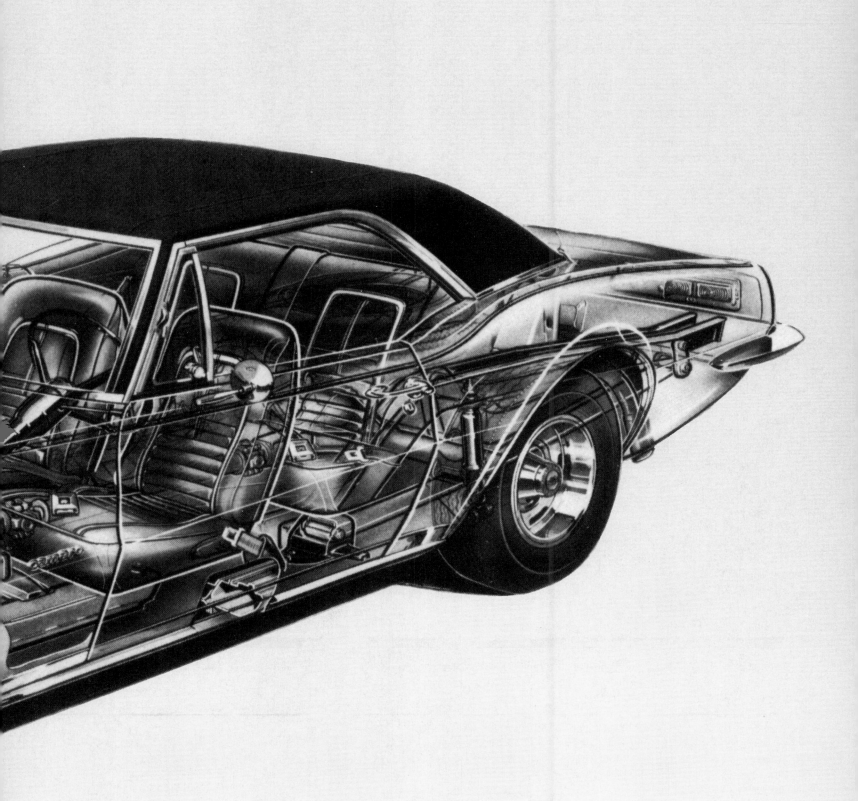

The 1967 Camaro in cutaway form.

While the designers were working on the visible parts of the new machine, the engineers were deep into the real problems, the working parts that make the exterior design more than just a beautiful concept. GM threw a lot of dollars, a lot of expertise, and a lot of experimental equipment and time into the Camaro program.

Heavy use was made of computers to work out the essential configurations and dimensions; computers also produced actual prototype parts by controlling production machinery. But they didn't start entirely from a blank sheet, work had already been going on to improve the Chevy II. This design had a unibody construction and work on it evolved a new style of construction, a style that was to prove controversial. This was a combination of the unibody style with a separate frame. The front skeleton of the car was to be a ladder frame bolted onto a rear unibody section. Front suspension was a combination of wishbone, structural cross member and tube/coil shocks; the rear utilized a system already used on the Chevy II, monoplate springs supporting a solid rear axle. These springs were splayed to allow room for a fuel tank capable of holding up to 18 gallons. The mixed style of suspension was to be controversial, but in 1965 it was a satisfying and cost-effective solution.

In mid-1965 the design came together in the first prototypes for the 1967 launch. Pete Estes had now taken over from Bunkie Knudsen. The car was advanced enough in essentials for even camouflaged models with card covers over the unfinished front and rear to cause excitement on the rare public test runs. As Estes was to say later, the Camaro "was a hot car, right from the start," and those who saw the disguised test cars in public also sensed that these low, slim vehicles were something special.

Of course there were problems, a major one being with the convertible which had a serious torsional shake fault. This was engineered out by using counterweights, a technique that certainly worked but which drew strong criticism from Estes.

A great benefit of the computer-aided design was that the new car had better handling than the wilful Mustang, assuring the driver of a predictable response which increased the safety margin of the car considerably. The computer had also designed the suspension, giving a more comfortable ride than the often bumpy experiences of Mustangers.

For greater safety there was a steering column capable of collapsing, a back-up hydraulic braking system, brake warning lights, hazard indicator lights, and an optional front seat safety-belt fitting.

Because of the existing Chevrolet engine range the driver of the new car could choose from these:

      230-cu in six (140 hp)
      327-cu in V8 (210 hp)
      250-cu in six (155 hp)
      327 4bbl V8 (275 hp)

In addition there was a brand new engine especially for the Camaro range. This was a 350 4bbl V8 rated at 295 hp destined for the SS high-performance option. All these power units could have either three- or four-speed shift, or automatic transmission, designated "Powerglide." Larger engines had dual exhaust systems and all exhausts had transverse-mounted mufflers.

The Camaro designers were obliged to allow for the wide variety of wheel and tire sizes in stock. They came up against a problem that had both design and handling implications. Of course they had to allow space for the largest tires, but when they put the smallest tires and wheels into the prototype arches "it looked so bad we were just sick about it." Both they and the engineers were very keen on the larger tire concept, it improved

Above: *At the time of the launch, Pete Estes was general manager.*
Below and facing page: *Prototype parts, computer designed, and engines are tested by engineers.*

handling and gave that performance edge they wanted, but they met resistance from management and even marketing executives. As engineer Paul King was to put it, many Chevy executives "were not really fascinated with the importance of Chevrolet's being in the performance market".

There was also an accounting argument against bigger wheels and tires, and the designers and engineers just had to live with the problem. As design chief Hank Haga said about the effect on the Camaro, "it looked like a car on roller skates."

In many people's opinion this was the only serious design fault of the new car. But tires were 7.35 × 14s on five-inch rims. However there was an option for all Camaros, a wide oval red-stripe D70 × 14 on six. This was standard on the SS models.

Additional wind-tunnel tests carved small refinements off the existing shape of the front fender area giving the whole machine an enviable stability when in motion.

Standard Camaros had headlamps and inner parking lights, the Rally Sport (RS) and the Super Sport (SS) both had full-width grilles with no lights visible where they were expected. Park lights were on the valance under the bumper on these models. On the RS and SS the portions of grille in front of the headlights pivoted sideways under electrical power. They could also be operated manually.

The Super Sport option with more powerful engine had a raised hood center to accommodate the extra power, the "bumblebee" nose-stripe, an oval steering wheel, and optional fold-down back seat.

The Camaro was set to go, it had been tried, tested, tweaked, bullied, wheedled and molded into shape. Come early 1966 things were ready to roll, the Camaro seemed ready. But it was not, for at this late date it still had no name.

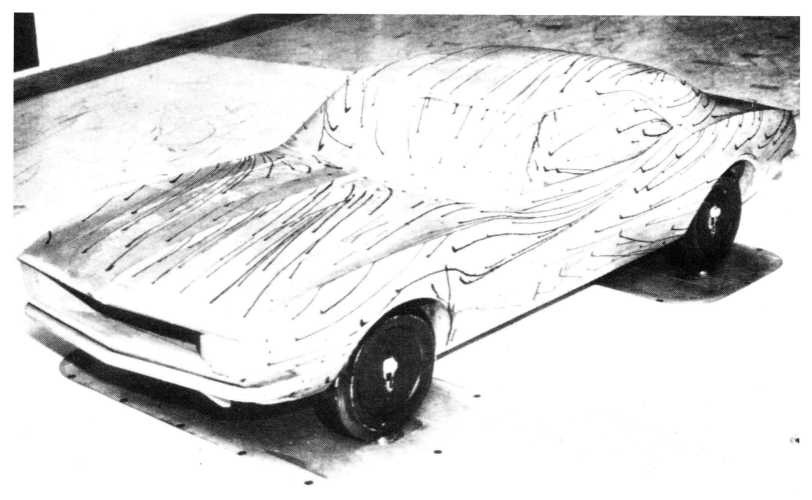

Above: *A prototype before an on-road development test in the winter of 1965–66.*
Facing page, top: *Paul King, in charge of passenger car engineering development at the proving ground.*
Left, and this page, top: *A quarter-scale model under test in the sound tunnel in 1965. The dark streaks show direction of the air-flow.*

WHAT'S IN A NAME?

The 1967 Convertible and the SS-350 Coupé feature in an early advertisement.

A car can be built from the road up and be completely new in every detail. It's rare for this to happen but it is possible. Most production cars have to take advantage of many existing production components in order to produce them at a price people can understand. The Camaro was no exception. It was certainly new, excitingly new, and the world of motoring waited eagerly to see what GM's challenger to the Mustang would be like. There was speculation about the new car, some of it accurate and intelligent. What no one ever guessed was the name. This was because no name had been decided upon.

If it were truly possible to build a name in the same way you build a car, and come out with something that sounds good and has the right kind of associations and is understood, then Chevrolet would have done so. The problem with car names is that they are loaded with emotion, they are more than abstract terms, more than sounds.

Mustang was a great name, it had all the right associations, and so it was natural that some animal name would be considered for its rival. Chevrolet went as far as tooling two animal possibilities, "Panther" and "Wildcat."

They also considered incorporating the letters GM in a name and came out with G-Mini which became GeMini and finally Gemini. The name was discarded, not because of the obvious fact that Gemini means "Twins," a most peculiar name for a car, but because they were forbidden to use the letters GM in case the car was a failure, and GM were not about to be associated with any kind of failure!

Chevrolet had got into the habit of using car names beginning with C. After an enormous amount of trouble they came up with "Camaro."

It was considered to be a good name because no one knew what the hell it meant, its anonymity and slightly exotic flavor made it win out over five thousand rivals.

Its meaning was "friend," "companion" and it had both Spanish and French associations. It had other meanings as well, one of which was a species of crawfish . . .

There had been a lot of media speculation about the new car,

most of it using the name *Panther,* so Chevrolet decided to announce the real name in advance in late June 1966. In so doing they risked the delight of Ford who soon found out that the Spanish meanings included "a shrimp-like creature."

There was doubt also over the spelling, the announcement had been at a phone-linked press conference, "Camaro" is pronounced "Camairo" and papers ran stories announcing the new car as "Camero."

Then one journalist found another Spanish definition, "loose bowels." All sorts of controversy hit the fan. It was publicity all right, but not what GM had hoped for.

When the car was launched in September, however, GM were able to point out that the softly rounded shape of the new car had a gentle sounding name and thus they were able to counter the stern criticism by the safety lobby which was loudly against aggressive performance and macho images. The press and posters featured shots of women as well as men driving the car. People soon forgot the dubious alternative meanings of the word.

As the arguments drifted on, the real facts about the car began to make their impact; it was to be priced below its Mustang competitor at all levels from base car up to V8 hardtop, and it had a page-long list of advantages over the Mustang including better handling, more road contact with wider treads, more safety features, more comfort, more engine-drive train variations, more corrosion resistance, safer brakes, more external variations, better trim and upholstery, acrylic lacquer finish, power windows, folding seats, and other options. All this for a lower price.

Things looked set for "the most interesting sales race in automotive history."

Press stories on the new car were enthusiastic – "a tasteful American interpretation of the European Gran Turismo."

Two aspects of the launch, with Pete Estes holding the lighted match, and cars ready for the press reception.

What the public and media didn't know was that Chevrolet had already planned a further assault on Ford, this time on the race-track where the Mustangs had been romping home as a result of Ford's decision to support racing openly. This was in defiance of the 1957 SCCA ruling against factory sponsored teams. Chevrolet had been supplying parts and facilities to private teams, despite a firm GM ban on helping such private racers. The new Trans Am series demanded a 305-cu in (5-liter) maximum displacement engine. Now Chevy planned to build a new engine to make the Camaro a Trans Am car. This was to be known in the future as the Z28 Camaro.

Chevrolet rapidly put together a tuned transmission, adapted chassis and an engine derived from production parts, a 327 block, a 283 crankshaft to create a 302-cu in displacement power unit. Because the first engine tried out successfully was the 283, the new car was to be known as the Z28. This was in fact the title of an existing option for the Camaro but fitted so well that they slapped it on the new machine.

When the Z28 was shown at Riverside, California in November it promised the new 302. Technically this meant a tuned runner intake manifold, the 800 CFM Holley four-barrel carburetor with closed positive ventilation, dual drive pulleys for fan and water pump, exhaust valves 2.02-in intake and 1.6-in outwards flow, high rpm distributor points, and dual exhaust ports. Suspension was heavy duty. Drive train was close-ratio four-speed with 2.2 to 1 ratio in low gear and 3.73 : 1 ratio on rear axle. Front braking discs were power assisted and the manual ratio on the steering was 24: 1. Tires would be 7.35 × 15 red-stripe. A rear spoiler and vinyl top were promised as options.

In order to make the Z28 qualify for the race series, each component had to be produced in quantities laid down by the FIA. The Chevrolet Engineering team responsible had to design, make, test, produce, and clear the parts that would turn the "tractable street carriage into a full-bore competitor." Time was so short that the special racing-duty parts were shipped direct to dealers and even to racetracks. The first Z28 production unit car emerged two days before the year 1966 began, and Roger Penske, racer and Chevy dealer, took delivery of his Z28 on January 10, 1967 in order to rebuild it for the Daytona race on January 30. Despite the crazy time scale Penske and three other Z28 drivers turned up for the Daytona race. Penske's Camaro, after leading the race, was withdrawn with engine problems. The real hit of the race was the Canadian Craig Fisher who

Facing page: *The Z28 revised 302 V8 engine.*
Top: *This 1967 RS/SS Convertible was an Indy 500 pace car.*

Meet the masked marvel.

Meet Camaro. Masked because it carries Rally Sport equipment with hideaway headlights. A marvel because it's an SS 350: telltale domed hood, rally stripe and Camaro's biggest V8. Over 3,200 pounds of driving machine nestled between four fat red-stripe tires, an SS 350 carries the 295-horsepower 350-cubic-

inch V8. So you know it's some other kind of Camaro. For a suspension, it has special high-rate springs—coil in front, single-leaf in back—and stiffer shocks at all four corners. And with its exceptionally wide 59" tread, we assure you an SS 350 handles the way a sporting machine should. And for your added safety,

every Camaro—be it SS 350 or not—comes with such protective conveniences as the GM-developed energy-absorbing steering column, dual master cylinder brake system with warning light, folding front seat back latches and shoulder belt anchors. Try one on at your Chevrolet dealer's. It's a ball-and-a-half.

Above and left: *Advertisements for the 1967 Sport Coupé and the SS350.*
Following pages: *The 1967 SS350.*

brought his hastily adjusted Z28 in at second place. It was a triumphant result, for Fisher's Camaro had elbowed aside Dan Gurney (Cougar) Parnelli Jones (Cougar) and Jerry Titus (Mustang). Three Camaros entered the Daytona 24-hour race, begun on the same day, and put in a good showing. None of them finished, however, as they were all using heavy-duty parts under conditions that had never been tried before, with speeds of up to 162 mph (260 km/h) being achieved.

After these events Chevrolet Engineering had a load of tortured and battered parts to investigate and learn from. The biggest problem had been rear wheel locking under braking and Penske suggested the addition of an adjustable rear brake pressure regulator.

Early in 1967 there was a verbal battle in the media when it was announced that the Camaro had been chosen to pace the Indianapolis 500. This was contrary to AMA regulations, and contrary also to General Motors' known policy about racing involvement.

MAKING TRACKS

Early on in the Camaro program there had been a definite split in Chevrolet's thinking. Anyone entering the small car market eventually came to this problem: was their car to be a true sports car, or a muscular race car? Or something in between? The European concept of the two-seater had never been very suitable for the wide open spaces and long roads of the United States, and a back seat of some kind had always been necessary. But the problem had never really been solved. Chevrolet took both roads. It produced cars for the street and it produced cars for the track. And it did so under the constant pressure from safety and ecological lobbies to tame down the performance of cars.

Outwardly Chevy took the soft approach, rounded lines, names that didn't evoke images of wild savagery or predatory beasts, a marked effort to appeal to women drivers and, in principle, agreement with GM's policy to keep out of the prize-fight ring of racing. But there was nothing to stop Camaro owners from entering races, and Chevy's unspoken policy was not to get in their way. In reality Chevy was doing all it could to help Camaro racing short of writing blank cheques for the racing teams.

The Indy pace car, the Z28, the production of heavy duty parts were all expressions of Chevrolet's racing interest, and in many senses racing was desirable. First of all it provided grueling tests for the Camaro, then it gave the car public prominence. Though it was against the rules no one could blame Chevrolet for their attitude, for in 1962 Ford announced they would support racing openly and began shifting large sums of money towards the race game.

Chevrolet took early benefit from their early failures on the race track, while not winning races they were tightening up the inevitable faults in the machine and getting more frequent public reaction. Supplying the Daytona Pace car involved a huge operation, with a massive and expensive support and publicity facility, plus a hundred replicas, a fleet of support vehicles, mobile workshops and all the ballyhoo of a prestige event. Yet despite all this the Chevrolet top brass remained obscure about racing involvement. "We don't think racing is economical or necessary," was GM Board Chairman Fred Donner's reply to a public question. Pete Estes merely said, "I've got to go along with the boss." So why all the Indianapolis pizzaz? "Indy exposure is good for any product," replied Estes demurely.

Demure was the image of the car, but the sales figures were aggressive at over 100,000 in the first seven months of release. The Camaro had taken a bite out of Mustang's rump and Ford winced. The youth market had been wooed persuasively by

clever advertising, they had looked at the Camaro, had accepted offers to test drive it, and they had begun buying it, often in preference to the mighty Mustang.

The main engineering problems encountered were with weight and the braking system. Other manufacturers had been suspected of acid-dipping to shed pounds from their supposed factory models and it was known that the Camaro could do with being lighter. There was also rear-axle hop under braking the loss of front system pressure. These were examined closely for the future.

Vince Piggins, product promotion manager closely involved with racing, recommended lighter body panels and ordered an intensive brake test program.

Come May new rear axle ratios were released, these were 3.23:1, 3.42:1, 3.90:1, and 4.33:1. Now Camaros could be finely tuned for the different race surfaces they were encountering, fine tuning that could mean a lot in competitive driving. But weight was still the problem, some Camaro drivers claiming as much as a 500 lb (227 kg) disadvantage. Fisher-Body came up with lightweight panels that shed 95 lb (43 kg).

Left: *A 1967 Convertible.*
Above: *A 1966/67 prototype.*
Right: *Vince Piggins, the product promotion manager.*

The brake problems were mostly solved by discovering that the brake bias valve, the same as that used on the Corvette, had been hooked up backwards throwing most of the load onto the rear. This caused the hop.

While Camaros had been making their impact on the roads and race tracks (third place in the overall Trans Am series in 1967) the hot rodders had seized on the Camaro with grunts of delight. Dan Chevrolet of California shoehorned a 427 engine into a Camaro, squeezed on the biggest slicks possible and produced a package that *Motor Trend* tested; they said, "No matter how many hot cars you've driven, the first time you really uncork a Dana Camaro you're bound to be awe-stricken if not outright panicked at the sheer magnitude of the forces unleashed." MT recorded a quarter mile time of 12.75 seconds at 110 mph (177 km/h).

The 427 Camaros tested on the road performed excellently on the open stretch but were found to be awkward in town traffic. All in all, the Camaro had made a good start in 1967, sales for the year were 201, 134. For a brand new car in a competitive market this was good going by anyone's standards. Ford had begun to look over their shoulder.

Right: *Another 1967 Convertible.*
Below: *The 1967 Convertible interior.*
Right, below: *The 350ci fuel-injected engine.*

THE MAIN ATTRACTION

echanically the 1968 Camaro was vastly improved over the previous year, but on the surface there was apparently little change; slight alterations to the lights and molding signposted some improvements to the engines and chassis.

The Camaro looked soft, but inside it was as tough as any of its competitors. The Z28 had a revised 302 engine and a close-ratio heavy-duty transmission, the M-22. Homologations for the Trans Am race series included twin four-barrel carbs, all round disc brakes and a wider front valance to combat aerodynamic lift. The Z28 was a powerful and affordable muscle car package at about $400 more than the standard Camaro coupé. And of course all the Trans Am homologated parts were available for the street Z28.

Late fall 1967 saw the first tryouts of the race Camaros. Smokey Yunick was to continue development work for Vince Piggins, while the Penske team of Mark Donohue and Craig Fisher benefited from input from Terry Godsall, the Canadian manager. Chevrolet gave the Penske team engineering expertise and there was Sunoco sponsoring. Penske stiffened up the chassis of the race Camaros. Early 1968 saw a Camaro-Mustang duel at the Daytona 24-Hour in the Trans Am class. The results were solid but not brilliant, all the Camaros losing pit time. The following month the Camaros came in first and second in their class and overall third and fourth in the Sebring 12-hour enduro.

In April 1968 Chevrolet announced the twin four-barrel cross-ram Z28 induction system, a veritable blast in the eye for the anti-performance lobby. This system was to create a resonant effect that would send precise wave peaks of fuel-air mixture into the inlet valve at the time of opening. This was designed to fit into the hood by special ducting that came as part of the conversion kit. It was of course meant for the track. Chevrolet rated this modification at 280 bhp at 5800 rpm, but *Road & Track* magazine reckoned it to climb to an incredible 350 bhp at 6200 rpm. Zero to 60 mph (96 km/h) was clocked at 6.9 secs, the quarter at 14.9 secs. at 100 mph (160 km/h). Top speed was 132 mph (212 km/h).

It was natural that the Z28 should be measured against its arch-rival, the Mustang. The heavier Camaro and the specially-wheeled Mustang gave each other a fair fight. On the drag strip the Camaro clocked 13.77 secs, the Mustang 13.96 secs. Camaro speed was 107.39 mph (172.82 km/h) on the run and the Mustang did 106.13 mph (170.79 km/h). Stopping distance from 80 mph (129 km/h) was 209 ft (64 m) for the Camaro and 248 ft (75.6 m) for the Mustang. The Mustang was faster on the circuit doing the 1½ miles (2.4 km) in 1:08.8 against the Camaro's 1:09.2. The Camaro did the zero to 60 mph (96 km/h) acceleration in 5.3 secs, the Mustang in 5.4 secs. Top speeds were 132 mph (212 km/h) for the Camaro and 131 mph (210 km/h) for the ponycar rival.

There were some pungent criticisms of the Camaro, still in its early days, the old rear-axle hop was still there, the four-speed shift linkage was criticised, as was the general stiffness of the ride, but the brakes came in for high praise from a variety of sources, and the power steering was also highly appreciated.

Previous pages: The 1969 SS Coupé.
Top right: *1968 Camaro Trans Am.*
Right: *The Camaro at Sebring in 1968.*
Facing page: *At Daytona in 1968.*

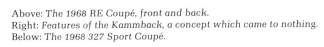

Above: *The 1968 RE Coupé, front and back.*
Right: *Features of the Kammback, a concept which came to nothing.*
Below: *The 1968 327 Sport Coupé.*

The race results in the improved Z28 were very satisfying, Donohue drove his Penske team Z28 to ten wins in thirteen events and the series title was taken by Chevrolet. Mustang scored two. The credit for these wins must be down to teamwork, but the modest Vince Piggins credits Donohue for working at the best balance regarding suspension.

Planned and canned for the 1969 restyle were a Kammback station wagon (too expensive to produce) and a fastback (thumbs-down from management who had burned their fingers on fastbacks in other series). So the design team went back to the drawing board, leaving the wild custom looks and performance to dealers like Baldwin Chevrolet who got out a dyno-tuned model with Super-Bite suspension and worked it up to what was known as the Baldwin Phase III SS-427. This was reckoned to turn 120 mph (193 km/h) in 11.5 secs, just as long as you were a qualified driver on an NHRA strip. These opulent goodies were for the real buffs, but there were enough drivers wanting the Camaro to take the year's production figures up to

Above: *A 1967 fastback design.*
Right: *A 1969 advertisement.*
Below: *One of the 1969 models, the 327.*

235,147. Of this quarter million plus, 184,200 had the V8 and 7,199 were 302 V8s in Z28 models.

As a total restyle was planned for 1970, the 1969 Camaro was altered in the general direction of a harder image, responding to criticism that it looked too soft and rounded. In the designs the horizontal lines were emphasized, and there were to be wider wheel openings to accommodate more road-gripping rubber. A more aggressive look was achieved by horizontal lights, lines and grilles.

The inside instrumentation became squarer and more chunky looking, the seats were more comfortable, taking care of the stiff ride often experienced in previous years. The RS retained the hidden headlamp theme, SS models had a raised hood-center and wide oval tires. The Z28 reaped the race-track experience and came equipped with disc brakes on all four wheels. Extra engines available included an optioned 250-hp, 350-cu in displacement for normal fuel.

For the first time all models optioned the three-speed Turbo-Hydramatic transmission, plus a torque-drive automatic for the six-cylinder engines. The optional four-speed manual gearbox lost its Muncie linkage in favor of a Hurst shifter.

As if to play down the proven successes on the race-track there were still the cosmetic stripe options and the heavy emphasis on female drivers in the advertising material. Chevrolet was still pretending it didn't have anything to do with racing.

Not so the racing-keen designers and associated engineers under the guidance of Vince Piggins. Now that they had a proven basic machine they set about shaving and adding to its shape to give the Camaro racer less drag and more road-holding ability. The improvements were made out on the track, leapfrogging the complications of wind tunnel work. Their wind-tunnel was Daytona. From this practical work came the Z28's add-on rear spoiler and integral air-dam.

In January 1969 came the good news that Camaro would again pace the Indy 500. It would be a white SS396, 375 hp with Turbo-Hydramatic transmission. Special instrumentation and custom upholstery in black and orange houndstooth check material were featured on the inside. It was planned to sell replicas of the pace car.

After the Indy announcement came another success: NASCAR had also adopted the Camaro as its official 1969 pace vehicle.

As this was being announced Pete Estes was promoted and John De Lorean took his place, eager to push Mustang aside with the sales-climbing Camaro.

All this excitement was complemented by a story that Camaro would soon be supplied with a new Chevrolet engine, the revolutionary ZL1. This aluminum 427 power unit was planned to sit in a new design, all black, gold trim, large wheeled, dual exhaust beauty to be known, obviously, as the ZL1. It was intended purely as a drag racer, but everyone understood that it was squaring up to the Boss 429 Mustang. About seventy of these were built and, despite the fears and suspicions that they would eventually find their way onto the streets, they soon became prized collectors' items, too special to use as transportation.

Below: *Pete Estes, general manager, hands over to his successor, John De Lorean, in February 1970.*
Facing: *In the 1969 Indianapolis 500 the Camaro was the pace car.*

This 1968 Camaro RS has been modified privately. It is a good example of the extent to which enthusiasts will go to obtain the maximum performance — and more! — from their Camaros.

This SS is the third 1968 Camaro owned by young Mike Edwards but the only one of the trio to have completed a full season on the ultra-competitive ISCA show circuit.

Not long before these pictures were taken he had driven down 1,200 miles from Cincinnati, Ohio, to the event in West Palm Beach, Florida.

The centerpiece of the staggeringly detailed engine bay is an 0.30-inch overbored small-block, uprated by means of ported and polished Brodix aluminum cylinder heads, Milodon gear drive, Crane cam, dual 650 Holleys feeding a Weiand 6–71 blower, Vertex magneto and Cyclone headers.

The modifications of this 1968 SS are even more extensive than those carried out to the RS shown on the previous pages, including a heavy use of chrome in the engine and suspension.

Owned by Rich Johnson of St Petersburg, Florida, this 1969 Camaro RS-SS has undergone considerable changes in its life, first as a drag racer and then as a street machine. The latter transformation began with work undertaken by the owner on a new box-section frame for the rear end in order to narrow the width to accommodate monster tires. Up front, a tunnel ram manifold was mated to twin carbs and new block and cylinder head components, all of which made for a massive increase in horsepower. The Hurst Quarter Stick-shifted Turbo-Hydro 400 backing the big block made a potent powertrain.

Supplementary instruments, wheel well changes, a 6-point rollcage – and much, much more in its internal and external appearance – ensured the car's success in a number of prestigious events.

A 1969 Camaro RS-SS, which for several years was used for drag-racing, has been extensively modified in all "departments", from the upholstery to the engine. The result has been a winning combination in official club and association events as well as in the pleasure it has given its Florida owner.

The impressive 1971 Rally Sport.

CAMARO REVISED

The origin of the $70\frac{1}{2}$ Camaro lay in an attitude. Chevrolet wanted to be first in the sports car class. But Ford was in the way with its Mustang, and Chevrolet couldn't get past. What they really wanted to create was "the ultimate, a baby Corvette" according to Pete Estes. The desire and the skill were there, and the early drawings were drawings of dream cars, taper nosed, sleek, low, with prominent wheel arches full of wheel.

But these designs were never to come off the paper. As was usual, the concept was put out to two different studios; both groups were trying to design a no-frills purity of line, a car to last, not a two-year throwaway. But when their combined design got to the upper echelons, the sports car concept was chopped, bulked, twisted, and tweaked every which way.

The designers tried again, and stubbornly kept to their first ideals of what excitement in a car should really mean. But Bill Mitchell, VP of design staff, saw the similarity of its front end to the Nova and said no, do it over. He gave them a lead, and the snaky front end was introduced. So almost by accident the keynote of the new car was introduced, and it was a good-looking cue, for it gave the front end an angularity and sense of attack that the original soft, bumblebee nose certainly lacked. Six months after that a fiberglass mock-up was ready.

Because of the lateness of the 1970 launch, the new car (for it was a drastic redesign) was later to be known as the $70\frac{1}{2}$ the 70 model in reality being a hardly-changed 1969 Camaro.

Top: *William L. Mitchell was VP in charge of design for the second generation.* Above: *The 1970 Camaro SS.*

Facing page: *These drawings show the revised dimensions, layout and construction of the $70\frac{1}{2}$.*

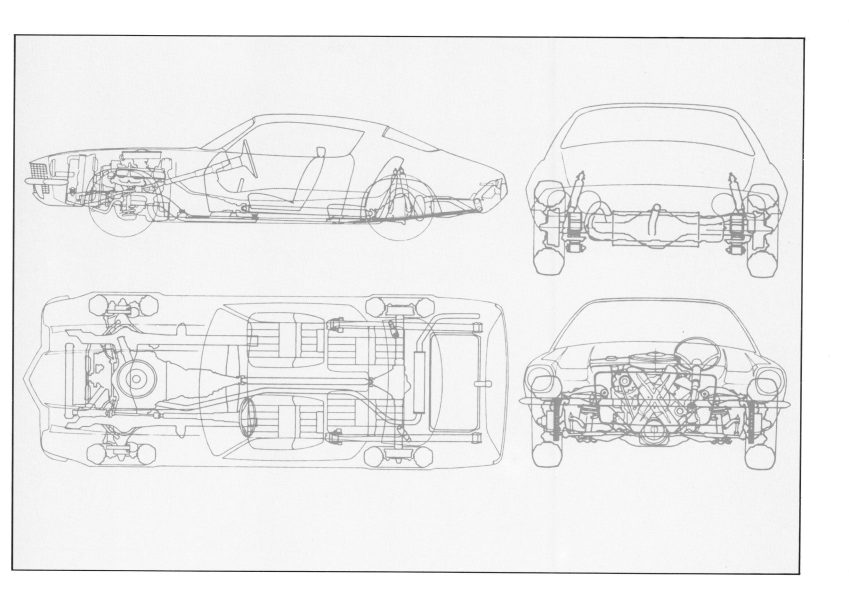

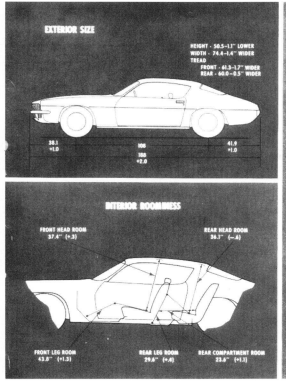

EXTERIOR SIZE

HEIGHT - 50.5-1.1" LOWER
WIDTH - 74.4-1.4" WIDER
TREAD
FRONT - 61.3-1.7" WIDER
REAR - 60.0-0.5" WIDER

38.1
+1.0

100
188
+2.0

41.9
+1.0

INTERIOR ROOMINESS

FRONT HEAD ROOM
37.4" (+.3)

REAR HEAD ROOM
36.1" (-.6)

FRONT LEG ROOM
43.8" (+1.3)

REAR LEG ROOM
29.6" (+.4)

REAR COMPARTMENT ROOM
23.6" (+1.3)

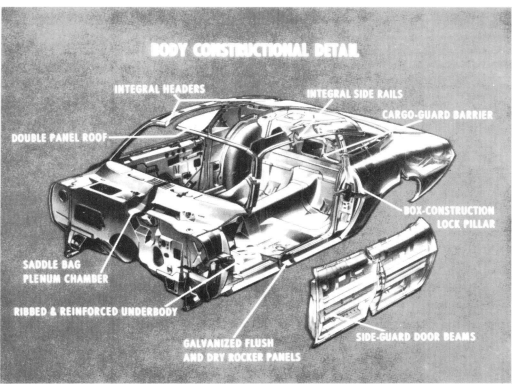

BODY CONSTRUCTIONAL DETAIL

INTEGRAL HEADERS

INTEGRAL SIDE RAILS

DOUBLE PANEL ROOF

CARGO-GUARD BARRIER

BOX-CONSTRUCTION
LOCK PILLAR

SADDLE BAG
PLENUM CHAMBER

RIBBED & REINFORCED UNDERBODY

GALVANIZED FLUSH
AND DRY ROCKER PANELS

SIDE-GUARD DOOR BEAMS

Early in 1970 John De Lorean claimed that Chevrolet would give an entirely new direction to the ponycar market with the new-design Camaro.

The Camaro was already an attractive car to first time buyers and 40 percent of those who purchased it were in this category. The industry average was 22 percent. De Lorean quite rightly saw this as an open door for future sales of other Chevrolet products. The Camaro had caught a large slice of the under 25 market and over half of its buyers had been single people. Women drivers tended to like the Camaro well enough to buy it for themselves. In fact they accounted for a quarter of Camaro sales.

Base priced at $2,749 the new Camaro certainly looked exciting with its pointed hood and stylish body lines that gave the car looks far higher than its price bracket. In addition it offered concealed windshield wipers as standard on the RS and SS and optional for other models, 10 percent more glass area, longer, more stylish doors with flush door handles, sloping foam-upholstered bucket seats, semi-bucket rear seats, a totally redesigned instrument panel, sound insulation, front disc brakes as standard, optional power steering, more efficient all round suspension, a 19-gallon gas tank, and a redesigned and engineered front sub-frame.

Engines on offer were the standard: 155-hp 250-cu in six, 200-hp 307 V8 plus a 250-hp 350; the SS: 300-hp 350 as standard and a 350-hp 396 as an option; and the Z28: 360-cu in 350 rating 406-hp. Other more powerful engines became available later for the Z28. Powerglide transmission was optioned in the less expensive models and standard for the power machines, and there was the usual choice of speeds, auto and manual.

The new Camaro had such sensational looks that it immediately became a choice for those who wanted "a Corvette for everyday use." The family resemblance was unmistakable.

Media and press reactions were good, the new car was hailed by *Car and Driver* as the "first of a new generation of American GT cars" and went on to praise both it and its cousin Firebird as "exceptional automobiles." The Camaro was praised for its feeling of interior space despite its fastback shape, and the new Z28 350 engine was greeted as an improvement on the old 302. The press also noted the resemblance to classic Ferraris and Maseratis and praised the new handling qualities. *Motor Trend*

Left, top: The 70½, as launched in February 1970.
Left, below: *The Sport Coupé version.*
Right: The new emblem on the 70½.
Below: *The 1970 Rally Sport had many newly designed features, including the instrument panel and headlamps.*

tested the four-speed Z28 and clocked zero-to-sixty at 7.0 seconds and the quarter mile at 14.9 at 97 mph (156 km/h), *Sports Car Graphic* got zero-to-sixty in 8.7 secs and the quarter at 15.3 secs doing 87.6 mpg (141 km/h) and added high praise for the feeling of being part of the car obtained from added leg room. *Hot Rod* clocked a quarter at 14.93 secs at 97 mph (156 km/h) with a passenger aboard.

But work on the Camaro was not over for that year. New SCCA Trans Am rules required that rear aerodynamic parts be production items to qualify for inclusion on race cars. Something had to be done fast, so Piggins snitched the center section of the Pontiac Firebird rear spoiler and set about adding end caps. Tests showed just how effective the new taller spoiler was, as it gave 168 lbs (76 kg) downforce at 116 mph (187 km/h), whereas the small spoiler tests resulted in 112 lbs (51 kg) uplift at that speed. Race Camaros just had to have the taller ducktail.

Production at short notice was a nightmare, for the first series race was scheduled at Sebring in March. There were big plans afoot for Camaro racing in 1970. A lot depended on it.

Homologation plans required many more production Z28s than it was thought Chevrolet could build in the time available. But exercising skill and ingenuity they managed to achieve what was conceived as impossible and their efforts were rewarded. The spoilers were approved for the next event.

Sales did very well and production was increased to 1,150 units a day, there were three full shifts working and it was planned to let them go right on through the mid-summer break because little retooling was going to be necessary for 1971. In April 1970 it was then currently outselling all its rivals.

In summer, *Sports Car Graphic* ran a comparison with the Corvette and found that the two cars turned in much the same results. Identical performance was recorded on top speed, 120 mph (193 km/h), braking deceleration, 0.86 g, skidpad acceleration, 0.76 g. This time the Z28 under test did zero-to sixty in 6.5 secs and the quarter in 14.6 secs at 98.3 mph (158 km/h). The Z28 actually outclassed the Corvette by showing only 2.8 degree of roll on the pad as opposed to the two-seater's 4.0 degrees. SCG still found time to complain about the notorious Camaro rear axle hop, even after those results! You can't please all of the people all of the time.

On the future design side John De Lorean introduced what was called the K-body project. The idea, simple like all good ideas, was to combine all Chevrolet's small cars onto one common platform. This unibody could have been lengthened or shortened but its introduction would save millions of dollars otherwise devoted to separate tooling.

Camaro would be involved of course and the advance models developed into a fastback and another attempt at a Kammback sport-wagon variation. They were always trying to get that Kammback into production. But then Ed Cole strangled the project and there was no Kammback at all.

Also in a dark mood was Vince Piggins who witnessed Ford's stock-block small V8 roll merrily home ahead of the race Camaros. He begged GM management to build a Chevy small-block engine with valves and ports comparable with the Ford engine's bigger sizes. But there were priorities other than an expensive racing engine, there was a recession in the auto industry which resulted in cut-backs on what were seen as low priority development programs. The race year ended with Ford taking the Trans Am series with 72 points, AMC came second with their Javelin scoring 59 points and Chevy had to be content with a third placing at 40 points. End of model year 70½ gave sales figures of 148,301 and of these only 8,733 were Z28s. Mustang sold 170,000.

More gloom gathered on the horizon as these figures were announced; GM began a policy of slicing back compression ratios on all their engines to allow them to use low octane gas and rated horsepower figures were set to collapse all over. And there was a 70-day strike that hit hard at production figures and sales. Ford reaped the benefit, while cynics saw the end of the performance car in sight.

Left, top: *The 1970 Rally Sport.*
Left, below: *Two of the 1970 engine options were the 300 hp V8 and the 360 hp Z28.*
Top: *The 1970 Z28 had very attractive clean-cut lines.*
Right: *One of the designs for the K-body concept; a Kammback design was considered but again rejected.*

UNDER TENSION

utwardly the 1971 Camaro looked the same as the 1970½ model. That was mostly because it was the same, they even used old publicity stills again. But things had been happening under the undeniably stylish steel. Use of lower compression ratios to allow unleaded gas made it necessary to publish both gross and nett horse-power figures. Here they are:

250 cu in six 145 hp gross/110 hp net
307 V8 200 hp gross/140 hp net
2 bbl 350 245 hp gross/165 hp net
4 bbl SS 350 270 hp gross/210 hp net
SS 396 (ie 402) 300 hp gross/260 hp net
Z28 350 330-hp gross/275 hp net

It was quite something to have to admit.

Inside the car there was at least a two-position adjustable seat but as an option; a cushioned steering wheel and soft-topped controls answered new safety requirements. The only real change outside was an optionable air dam spoiler, plus the tall rear spoiler that had caused such agony the year before.

Not everyone accepted the fact that the new regulations threatened the performance car sector, and the indefatigable Vince Piggins recommended the development of a 400-cu in engine for the Z28. A prototype was made, tested and found to be "impressive and highly acceptable." It was a light-weight, high torque, low compression power unit that made a lot of sense. Unfortunately the economic climate was wrong and GM management decided against it.

Camaro had won itself a solid reputation as a stylish, affordable road car and it sold well, so well that many people predicted that it would outsell Mustang. But on the racetrack it

was going nowhere fast, and no factory cars were to be provided for that year's Trans Am series to help beef up the efforts of the privately entered Z28s.

It was safety standards, rather than race track times, that were on people's minds. The National Highway Traffic Safety Administration was determined to make road driving safer and introduced the first federal bumper standards which would be obligatory on 1973 models. Attractive design solutions to the problem of having to add extra material to the front end included the "soft-nosed" concept, body color bumpers in impact resistant materials that gave the look of there being no bumpers at all. The effect was handsome, but there was a price tag to that way of doing things. But the design was ahead of its time, in fact almost without realizing it the designers had jumped ahead in time to what would be the 1978 Camaro look.

Reality, cost, the declining market, and anxious accountants all proved a formidable combination and the designers returned to the task of strengthening the existing bumpers. It had to be a considerable strengthening. Even as they worked on it there were people who were cynical about the chances of a 1973 Camaro even being produced. Sales were down to 116,627, over 31,000 less than the year before. And of these 116, 627 only 4,863 were Z28s. Camaro did not outsell Mustang, nor did it make any impression in the Trans Am series. The struggling independent teams didn't notch up a single victory between them.

Previous pages: *The 1971 Z28, very similar to the 1970 model except for detail changes.*
Below: *The SS Coupé of 1971.*

1972 reaped the bitter harvest of the sales slump. All development programs had been postponed or killed off. The Camaro was unchanged save for the necessary emission standards requirements and a number of small, half-hearted cosmetic options, a vinyl roof, a "sport" steering wheel and (would you believe?) a wider white stripe on the whitewall tires. It really did look as if the car was about to make its long last lonely drive to oblivion.

Not that this deterred the sales people. The Camaro was offered as a substitute for the Corvette, a four-seater sports car that could do everything the Vette could do at a lower price tag.

Another approach was to put together specialist packages. There was the "Budget GT" (yes, it's no misprint) which had the 350 V8 rated at a somber 165 hp, four-speed transmission, Positraction 3.08:1 axle ratio, F41 sports suspension, power brakes, power steering, rally wheels, bias belted tires, radio, and special instrumentation. Price $3,850. Budget, yes. But GT?

Then there was the "Luxury GT," same engine and line-up as before plus every option you could want, and probably some you didn't want: tinted glass, rear window defroster (oh those freezing Grosse Pointe mornings), air conditioning, clock (to save you looking at your watch), tilted steering wheel and custom upholstery. $4,365. *Road & Track* liked the air conditioning.

Then there was the "Performance GT," which was a Z28 with automatic transmission, 4.1:1 rear axle, tilt wheel, Rally Sport/custom interior. Oh, and a radio. $4,558.

Constant research and development are required, including handling (above), emission control to meet new regulations (facing page), and engine and chassis testing (left), using computers.

Budget, Luxury and Performance GTs were rated respectively:

	Budget	Luxury	Performance
Zero-to-sixty	9.8 secs.	10.5 secs.	7.5 secs.
Quarter mile	17.6 secs.	17.2 secs.	15.5 secs.
at	79 mph	82.5 mph	90 mph
	(127 km/h)	(133 km/h)	(145 km/h)
Top speeds	107 mph	110 mph	124 mph
	(172 km/h)	(177 km/h)	(199 km/h)

And that was that.

It was about this time, mid 1972, that the crises piled up to a point of decision. Harsh emission control and safety laws, new standards regarding damageability, oil crises, strikes, high development costs, duplication of effort, inflation. You name it. Because of its relatively small share in the total market of GM, the F-car series looked ripe, on paper at any rate, for a swift cancellation. New bumper standards were on the horizon and expensive redevelopment was another argument for cancellation.

Then the Camaro *was* cancelled. Ed Cole announced the decision. But the engineers and designers and others just wouldn't let go. They seized on the expensive bumper argument and worked like slaves to come up with a cheaper solution. By strutting and use of bumper guards they managed to get the standards met without expensive rejiggings. As Camaro chief engineer Bob Dorn said, "The RS looked like a NASCAR stock car, it had too many rods and struts behind those little bumpers."

The Camaro was indeed a beautiful car and well-made. "From the engineering standpoint it was the best car we had at the time, and it would have been illogical to cancel the best car we had," said Dorn. His view was supported by others and after a lot of words the Camaro was saved.

Having got this reprieve for the 1973 Camaro, the designers and engineers set about planning a better bumper solution for 1974. They decided on lightweight aluminum bumpers mounted on springs which would ease any impact and return the bumper to its original position. They also began designing a new series of rounded soft-fronts, and curved glass backs.

In the middle of all this frenzy and gloom came a shaft of sunlight, or maybe a streak of lightning. They put a turbo-charged six into the Camaro and compared its runs against a stock six. The Turbo Hydramatic job did the quarter in 16.8 secs at 86 mph (138 km/h) compared to the stock's 20.28 secs at 67 mph (108 km/h), and on a 50-70 mph (80-112 km/h) passing test it clocked 5.12 secs as compared to the stock time of 12.87 secs. But no one had any plans to do anything about it. The streak of lightning turned out to be a flash in the pan. Things didn't look too bright race-wise either; the independents made valiant unaided efforts but the result was a fourth overall place in the Trans Am series, with AMC hitting the top with twice as many points as Chevy.

Then there were the sales figures. A disastrous 171-day strike knocked sales way down to 70,809 with a paltry 2,575 Z28s included in that figure. For those who had worked hard and long on the car there was another blow; 2,000 half-completed Camaros and Firebirds stood marooned, unable to be sold because of the required 1973 safety, emission, and damage-ability standards. The idea of completing them and exporting them was canned, and the cars were hauled away to the crusher. It was hard to take.

Luckily the Camaro program was not itself to be crushed, Chevy had done well sales-wise in other models and the Camaro rode through disaster on this family profit. Camaro turned its back on 1972 with scars all over its mind, but it went into 1973 powerfully.

First off it began to aim at an older, richer market with a new model designated LT, Luxury Touring. It had everything on it, the 350 V8 power steering, dual remote control mirrors, special moldings, paint, trim, seats, insulation, instrumentation, and 14 × 7 Rally wheels.

Standard fitments for all Camaros now included sport steering wheel, new seat harness and newly designed pedals to increase leg-room, exhaust gas recirculation system (EGR), new floor shifter, and new alternator.

The optioned two-speed Powerglide was replaced by the Turbo Hydramatic transmission on the base six cylinder. Other new options were a new floor console, new wheel covers and GT style wheels and with the Z28 a 245-hp hydraulic-lifter 350 engine, a good-sounding air cleaner, and air conditioning.

In all there were five Camaro variations: Budget 2 + 2, Insurance Special Sports Car (low insurance premiums were a great inducement), Luxury Camaro, Super GT, Maximum Performance.

Above: The 1972 Camaro

Below: The 1972 Rally Sport.
Right: Two views of the LT Coupé 350 of 1973.

The engines offered were: 250 six (100 hp), 307 V8 (115 hp), 2 bbl 350 (145 hp), 4bbl 350 (175 hp), and the high-compression Z28 350 (245 hp).

Once more the Z28 won high praise for its handling and performance and looks. With greater lower-end torque the Z28 was still turning in commendable times: zero-to-sixty in 6.7 secs, the quarter mile in 15.2 secs at 95 mph (153 km/h and top speed of 123 mph (198 km/h).

On the race track new IMSA Camel GT rules won favor with the Trans Am organizers and allowed sports cars such as Corvettes and Porsches to compete. Camaro won two races of the six, Porsche two and Corvette two, which gave Chevy a long-awaited boost to first place. Sales also climbed again, thankfully, to 91,678 with the Z28s contributing 11,575 to the total.

The sky seemed to have cleared. But had it?

A striking view of the 1973 Z28.

THE BIG CLIMB

A very personal Camaro of the early 1970's.

ohn Zachary De Lorean had guided Chevrolet to victory over Ford in the years 1969 to 1973. Chevys had broken sales records by topping the three million mark two years in succession. Now Long John was elevated to the Fourteenth Floor of GM, a position in car makers' eyes but a short step from heroic status, and Jim McDonald took over. McDonald was to experience, in his first year managing Chevrolet, the traumatic experience of the Middle East Oil Embargo. As always De Lorean's timing had been exact.

In 1974 there were a whole lot more regulations to take into consideration. Federal rules covered new safety and emission standards, a system that interlocked seatbelts with the ignition and made it impossible to start the car without having first put on the seatbelt. New rules resulted in heavier vehicles and lowered fuel efficiency.

Camaro now sported its new spring-mounted bumpers, altering but not damaging its appearance. Sensors and indicators to measure the wear on brake pads were engineering innovations, there were new ball-joints for the front suspension, new batteries and new air conditioning. The capacity of the gas tank was raised to 22 gallons, power steering was supplied on all V8s and there were other minor, invisible, improvements and readjustments.

1974 saw the disappearance of the Rally Sport model. It was the RS model that had originally caused all the stir with its concealed headlights. "Look, Mom, no headlights" became "Look Mom, no RS."

The Z28, flagship of the Camaro fleet, was given eye-hitting stripes and hood and decklid graphics.

When the oil embargo hit there was panic. But the Camaro, although a performance car, was in fact smaller than most and had the edge in gas mileage over a lot of fat cats from the sedan class. Sales looked great, there was continuous production and plans were laid for turning another factory over to Camaro building.

Life was full of ironies. The Z28 was being praised in the press as "the best performance package on the market today" (*Cars*) while Chevy advertising was pushing the car's looks as its main asset and saying, "As long as you've got to go slower, you may as well do it in style."

Camaro designers began putting together ideas for a smaller sporty coupé, just in case of a hurried redesign as a result of the prevailing crisis. But work was also going ahead on the performance side, and a revamped shape with glassed-in headlamps, wheel flares, and soft fore and aft ends was made in clay. This was to become the Berlinetta.

Camaro came before the public eye in a big way when it supplied cars for the International Race of Champions, a televised race series created by Roger Penske. In 1974 Camaro replaced the Porsches that had been used the year before. The idea was to provide winter excitement by putting on a series featuring the supershoes and champs from different series, including Formula One. It all gave bite to the Camaro image.

Sales profited; the year end saw a figure of 135,780, with 13,802 of those being Z28s, an overall increase of over 44,000 units. This in a year of chaos when all the automotive companies were hanging out the laundry halfway down the strip. Camaro hadn't eliminated Mustang but it had survived, and with style.

In 1975 another huge hunk of metal was tossed into the balance against designers and engineers. Or more accurately a chunk of metal filled with expensive chemicals, the catalytic converter. GM decided to lead the way, or unlead the way since only unleaded gas could be used with this system designed to

Below: *The 1974 Sport Coupé 350.*

CHEVROLET MAKES SENSE FOR AMERICA

EXAMPLE: CAMARO LETS YOU LIMIT YOUR SPEED WITHOUT CRAMPING YOUR STYLE.

Car enthusiasts used to say that a good-looking car "looks like it's moving even when it's standing still." Today's Camaro owners know all about that. They also know how well Camaro moves when it's moving. Because the way it looks is the way it goes.

LOOK AND FEEL GOOD AT 55.

Camaro is a car that's designed to be a joy to drive. The stance is wide and firm. The handling is smooth and stable because of the forward-mounted steering system, the sophisticated suspension and the wide-tread tires and wide-rim wheels. The front disc brakes resist fade, water, heat and dust. Even the sleek new front end incorporates a new improved bumper system.

AS GOOD-LOOKING INSIDE AS OUT.

Make yourself comfortable. Camaro gives you full-foam Strato-bucket seats and door-to-door cut pile carpeting. A soft-rim four-spoke steering wheel and floor-mounted shift add to Camaro's sporty good looks. Flow-through ventilation is standard. Inside the doors, there are steel guard rails.

Overhead, a double-panel steel roof.

PRICED LESS THAN $3000.

Sound like a lot of car? It is. Sound like a lot of money? It isn't. In fact, at $2889.70,* the '74 Camaro 6 Sport Coupe is the lowest priced car in its class.

Camaro is available in 6- and 8-cylinder versions. Plus, there's the luxurious Type LT and the heavy-duty Z28.

Take the time to check out a new Camaro at your Chevy dealer's. As long as you've got to go slower, you may as well do it in style.

*Manufacturer's Suggested Retail Price, including dealer new vehicle preparation charge. Destination charges, optional equipment, state or local taxes are additional.

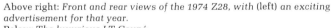

Above right: Front and rear views of the 1974 Z28, with (left) an exciting advertisement for that year.
Below: The luxurious LT Coupé.

meet hefty Federal emission requirements. The converter was a system of reducing noxious gases in the exhaust. In practical terms this meant fitting specially narrow filler tubes to all catalytic converter equipped cars, so that the normal wide nozzles of the leaded gas pumps could not be used. Special small-bore nozzles were fitted to pumps dispensing unleaded gas. It also meant a drop in fuel efficiency when coupled with the low compression engines. It was a good thing, perhaps, that the oil embargo lifted half way through the year.

The Camaro catalytic converters came as part of the High Energy Ignition System, an electronic system that gave a more intense spark; this came along with cooler air ducted in from outside the car and a system for warming up the gas to encourage speedier vaporization. It actually did result in some fuel economy and improved driveability on steel-belted radials, which were easier to shift along. The electronic ignition system and other refinements meant that service intervals were longer; for example, spark plug replacement was now only necessary every 22,500 miles (36,209 km) instead of the previous 6,000 miles (9,656 km). Camaro declared that its target was to

Left: *Designs for a more soft end.*
Above: *The Rally Sport came back as a paint and trim option early in 1975.*

Facing page, top: *It was a very attractive option and some 7,000 were sold.*
Facing page, below: *The Type LT Sport Coupé of 1976, front and rear.*

lengthen service intervals to 50,000 miles (80,465 km). But that was hopeful thinking.

The most attractive visual advance for 1975 was the rear wrap-around window, which added 10 per cent light and visibility and gave the impression of a triangular side window in back. There was a Sports Decor package, spots, mirrors, vinyl appliqués, also engine refinements, finned aluminum rear brake drums, and a muffler system for the V8.

What was of more importance, and some say it was a disaster, was that the redoubtable Z28, the style car for the series, was discontinued. Head-in-the-sand management was to blame, for it was soon to be obvious that there was a healthy market for performance cars despite the surrounding gloom. But by any standards it was a dumb thing to do.

Once more the wide interest in sports performance was ignored in promotional literature, and even the International Race of Champions (IROC) series, a gift for advertising and PR, was hardly recognized. In the IROC series Camaros were driven by a dozen of the world's best competitive champions with Bobby Unser taking the Daytona finale and title at an average speed of 167.5 mph (268.5 km/h).

Then, as if to say a belated sorry-sir, GM introduced a revived RS, now bedecked in all manner of bright colors and dripping with cosmetics in the shape of stripes, front and rear spoilers, and fancy mag-style wheels in body color. It was greeted by the press with a ho-hum of respect for its family, it was described as "relatively honest... not super bad, just competent." The press tried hard to be polite.

But what really spun the imagination and flared the nostrils of car buffs was a review of a race-style Camaro prepared under

the direction of Mark Donohue. It was a road version of the IROC racers. With a front spoiler like a cowcatcher it had Michelin tires on aluminum race wheels, tight suspension, cold air duct to the carb from the front, racing seats, fat-rim steering wheel, and air horns. The steering response was tight as a bow-string and one writer called it "a Camaro that behaves like a Ferrari." But it was a car that only a very few could ever hope to own with a price tag of $9,500. Still, it was an exciting preview of things to come. What the public did buy in 1975, however, were 135,102 Camaros. Perhaps with the Z28s that figure might have been higher.

Full production and additional volume with the Van Nuys plant on stream meant that the soft nose concept was established as a paying proposition. This was to give the designers a tremendous plus as the shapes for the coming years could be molded into exciting new aerodynamic sculptures. The future was within their ability to produce, and produce at a price that people could afford.

The distinctive front end of the Camaro, which had grown over the years into a strong, eager shape, was retained essentially unchanged for 1976. There were some slight adjustments to meet the rolling demands of emission regulations. With the base car still powered by the 250 six, the standard engine for all the rest of the line-up now became the new 2 bbl 305-cu in V8 designed for economy driving in the higher power range. These V8s came with power assist as standard, and newly introduced brake materials. Manual transmissions got a higher ratio: 2.85:1. The idea this year was to capitalize on a very attractive design, and the only significant new option was the cruise control for the LT. What had happened was very interesting, for the problem bumper requirements had been met in such a way as to give the front end the flexibility for future design which made the car look far more expensive than it really was. The soft front was a quiet revolution.

Benny Parsons   Brian Redman   James Hunt   Emerson Fittipaldi   Richard Petty   Jody Scheckter   A. J. Foyt   Mario Andretti   Bobby Allison   Al Unser   David Pearson   Bobby Unser (not shown)

Gentlemen, start your Camaros.

The third annual International Race of Champions is on.

Once again, in four fascinating events spread widely across the country and the calendar, 12 of the world's winningest drivers are competing in 12 identical cars, identically prepared. A true test of driving skill.

The cars are Camaros.

That should come as no great surprise. Camaro's aerodynamic shape makes it a natural for these events. The profile is low, the stance is wide, the size is right—and the feel is terrific. Drivers enjoy driving Camaros, people enjoy watching them.

Camaro has been a particularly popular off-road competition car ever since it was first introduced about 10 years ago.

Chevrolet salutes the 12 distinguished drivers of the third International Race of Champions.

Gentlemen, start your Camaros.

Chevrolet

WATCH FOR THE INTERNATIONAL RACE OF CHAMPIONS ON THE ABC TELEVISION NETWORK.

At last management gained the confidence to take full advantage of the IROC series with the unashamed announcement, "Gentlemen, start your Camaros", over a photo of the IROC Camaro surrounded by "the world's winningest drivers," Redman, Hunt, Fittipaldi, Scheckter, Foyt, Andretti, Al and Bobby Unser, Parsons, Petty, Allison, and Pearson. Chargers, champions and supershoes, the one picture said it all. As Bob Lund said, "The drivers loved the cars, we loved the races, and the public loved the races."

Now that the emphasis was back on excitement again there were plans to revive the foolishly-discontinued Z28. Pontiac had kept on the Firebird Trans Am, which was selling as fast as it could be produced. Other manufacturers were trying to give their cars the same image by throwing zingy paint schemes, racing stripes and all the other baubles at their underpowered machines.

The year ended on an upbeat; designers and engineers were producing great ideas for the new Z28 and a smaller, neater base Camaro, and sales for the year were 163,635, just behind the Mustang. And Joe Chamberlain scored a victory in one of the Trans Am races.

Above: This IROC picture featured in a 1976 advertisement and in the 1977 Camaro catalog.
Left: In 1974 Bob Lund took over as Chevrolet general manager from Jim McDonald.

News of the reborn Z28 was around as unconfirmed rumor at the time of the 1977 model introduction. That introduction saw new metallic colors for the RS package. Engines on offer were the standard six, 4.1-liter six, 5.0-liter V8 and 5.7-liter V8; tighter axle ratios meant more fuel economy, and in everywhere but California (state of sunshine and amazingly tough emission rules) horsepower ratings increased by an average of 5 hp per power unit. California Camaros were on average 5 hp lower than before and all cars for that state were automatic.

Come the Detroit Auto show in January 1977 the public were treated to a showcar tagged "Berlinetta," which had a bumperless soft front and rear, deep-recessed lamps in "sugar-scoop" placements, upper and lower egg crate grilles, integral front spoiler and flared fenders. Gold stripes on the outside complemented the hold-down pins, hood instruments in twin nacelles and a raised center section bearing the title "ZL1 Can-Am." Everyone knew that the unusual event of showing off the Berlinetta meant that Camaro had something coming, and a facelift was due for 1978. Then sneak preview photos of the 1978 model were seen: bar one or two details it was identical with the Berlinetta front.

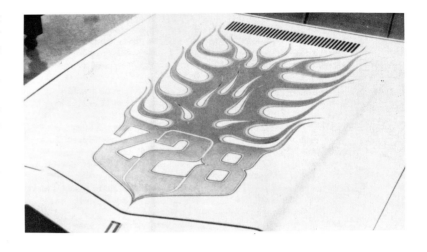

Above: *The Z28 decal seems to be vying with the Trans Am bird; the Berlinetta's (below) is much more restrained.*

Above: *The 1977 Type LT, with the exposed aluminum bumper.*
Right: *The Z28 comes back – a 1977 advertisement.*
Facing page: *Two years' absence – then the Z28 returns for its public debut at the 1977 Chicago Auto Show.*

But before that, in February 1977, at Daytona, the new Z28 was launched. Chevy made no excuses; "The Camaro Z28 is intended for the macho enthusiast . . . a special breed of aspiration car . . . aggressive, quick, agile, and dependable."

Although equipped with the 350 the Z28 gave much better performance because of its new engineering developments – the Borg Warner four-speed coupled to a high capacity clutch and a 3.73:1 rear axle ratio.

Turbo-Hydramatic was optional and gave a 3.42:1 ratio. Exhaust was cleaned by a large catalytic converter and then split to duo pipes whose small resonators gave the engine an attractive throaty tone.

A specially designed suspension system was a new introduction, a unique system incorporating stabilizer bars, spring rates, shock valves, and rear shackles. The car ran on GR 70-15 steel-belted radials and had a 14:1 steering ratio. Wheels and mirrors were body color, any of seven on offer, and grille and lamp bezels were blacked out. Decals and emblems included a duct-shaped hood appliqué. Price $5,170 and 60 cents.

Hot Rod magazine said: "a complete ball to drive . . . well-balanced . . . cohesive in responding to steering inputs . . . a terrific job." *Car and Driver* said: ". . . a road machine of the first rank . . . blitzed up the canyons and charged over the arroyos."

Straight line acceleration zero-to-sixty was 8.6 secs, the quarter mile in 15.35 secs at 91 mph (146 km/h).

Later in the year *Motor Trend* clocked zero-to-sixty in 8.0 secs and a 15.4 sec quarter mile at 90 mph (145 km/h). Bob Hall of that publication called it "the best-handling American production car I have ever driven." And there were more and more brilliant reports. The Z28 had returned with pride.

In 1977 another greater event was recorded for Camaro: for the first time it romped home ahead of Mustang sales. Camaro sold 198,755 to Mustang's 161,654. This figure included 14,347 of the new Z28s, so there could have been no more convincing proof of the hold the Camaro had on the minds of the driving public. And an even more exciting car was on the way.

KING CAMARO

The 1978 Camaro with the new front end design.

For eight years the basic Camaro body had remained essentially the same. The facelifts had indeed given the car an eager, thrusting character, and the engineering innovations had made it totally different. 1978 was to see the final facelift before the whole car was redesigned.

The sleekness of the car came from the body-color soft nose and rear, dispensing with old-fashioned metal fenders and there was now a trio of wide tail lamps.

Chevy now offered five Camaro models: the Sport Coupé, the LT, the RS (Rally Sport), the Rally Sport LT, and the Z28.

The Z28 now had a fake scoop to replace the decal, front fender louvers, and new stripes. In addition there was a T hatch roof with removable tinted glass panels, new aluminum wheels and a luxury interior.

Engine lineup consisted of the 4.1-liter six, the 5.0-liter V8 with new aluminum intake manifold, four-speed manual and a 3.08:1 axle ratio. The Z28 engine was uprated in horsepower to 185 hp. 5.7 V8s with automatic transmission were mandatory for California. New emission hardware included a re-use system of exhaust gases, and a charcoal filter.

Media coverage of IROC Camaros continued and the Camaro Z28 was dubbed 'His Majesty," outranking Mustang's "Boss" claim.

The new Z28 was tested by *Car and Driver* magazine and did the zero-to-sixty in 7.3 secs, quarter mile elapsed time was a straight sixteen and top speed 123 mph (198 km/h). Praise was unqualified "...the best rounded Z28 ever...ride, styling and interior comfort are all honed to a new brilliance."

King Camaro accompanied the quarter-century old 'Vette to the Indy 500 where fifty Camaros were on hand as official cars.

The advent into production cars in a serious way of the turbo started all manner of wild stories about Camaro's future. It was known that a redesign was in the air and some hinted at a turbo Z29. Others thought that the Camaro would be stopped completely.

A turbocharge package was made available in 1978, at a high price, from Bill Mitchell the engineer who had specialized in custom built Chevys. Only a few could possibly afford Mitchell's magic wand to be waved over their new Camaros, and there were a lot of new Camaros around in 1978. The two millionth came off the Van Nuys plant in May 1978, colored gold. It was the right color, for Chevy hit the mother lode in 1978 by selling 247,437 Camaros, of which an amazing 54,907 were Z28s. Mustang were trailing by nearly 70,000 units. There was a lot of truth in the claim that Camaro was king.

His majesty. The Camaro Z28.

Back in the Sixties, the Camaro Z28 was a car that could attract an auto buff on just about any street corner in America. It was a King. Now, it's back. And it's still a King.

For 1978, Camaro Z28 bears a sleeker, sharper look, with a new bump-resistant front end and color-coordinated rear bumper styling.

Some of its hardware: 1. 350 cu. in. 4-barrel V8. (Camaro is equipped with GM-built engines produced by various divisions. See your dealer for details.) 2. Dual exhaust pipes. 3. Special Instrumentation. 4. Close-ratio 4-speed. (Automatic transmission required in California.)

Camaro comes in several other spirited models. Each offers a new option—removable glass roof panels.

And each offers you that special Camaro road response. **Chevrolet**

Left, above: *Another Z28 advertisement – now for His Majesty!*
Left, center: *Official Indy 500 pace car in 1978.*
Left, below: *The lines of the 1978 Camaro.*

Above: *A Mitchell 1978 turbocharged Camaro and (below) one of the standard Camaros of that year.*

This success led to the retention of the 1978 Camaro into 1979. The LT was replaced by a new luxury car, the Berlinetta. The base six got a lower axle ratio of 2.56:1, the 5.0-liter V8 got a dualjet carb, and the Z28 got a front air dam that wrapped round to the front wheelhouses.

EGR (exhaust gas recirculation) technology had been striding ahead through necessity and its developments and those in ignition improved fuel economy and driveability.

The Z28 was now totally identified with the IROC series, no management worries about performance now. Past year IROC cars were now used as basic start platforms; one of these clocked zero-to-sixty in 5.2 secs and the quarter mile in 13.3 secs.

In 1979 233,802 Camaros were sold, slightly down but still a good performance, and it had begun to find popularity and sales even in Europe, an environment of motoring and design into which few American cars have ever successfully penetrated. The Camaro was small, stylish, and had superb performance, and these factors made it more acceptable to European conditions than the gas-guzzling giants of former years.

Top: *The luxury Berlinetta, introduced in 1979.*
Above: *The 1979 Z28 Sport Coupé.*
Below: *Another view of the 1979 Z28.*

Facing page: *The Z28 of 1979 had, as standard, new front air dams and bolt-on hood scoops.*
Below: *A turbocharged 350 engine.*

But by 1980 and another oil crisis, this time because of the Iranian revolution, the Z28, though recognized as a legend, had begun to attract a few short-tempered comments. Suspension was criticized and also "lack of efficiency"—whatever that may mean. It seemed a new tough realism had crept into the minds of the driving public, or at any rate into the minds of car reviewers. However it was favorably compared to others of its class.

Cars magazine, reviewing the 1980 Z28, pointed out that it equalled "fancy imports" at a much lower price tag, and quoted its zero-to-sixty run as 7.3 seconds and its quarter mile at 16.2 at 93 mph (150 km/h). It ended with the comment, "And the pure driving pleasure it continues to offer is a welcome reassertion of the human spirit in the teeth of emission-sniffing pusillanimity." Quite a phrase, but then the Z28 was quite a car. Metaphor-mangling apart, the critics strongly advised Chevy not to shoehorn the Pontiac 4.9-liter power unit into the Z28, as they had actually thought of doing.

The airdam on the 1980 Z28 was emphasized by striping, there was a solenoid-operated cold air intake on the hood with the words AIR INDUCTION in the same stripy style and the cast-aluminum wheels sported steel-belted radials with white lettering. Other models remained as before.

Unfortunately sales limped badly in 1980 at 131,066. The Camaro, though king, was not immune to the dark days of crisis-ridden 1979-80.

Californians however were treated to a little cheering news: they would be allowed to have the four-speed manual transmission at last and also the 5.7-litre V8. GM engineers had worked hard to get these certified for California's Draconian emission laws and had come up with an engine computer system—Computer Command Control—that regulated the combustion process.

Above: *In 1979 and 1980 this Ultra Z concept car inspired a great deal of approving comment.*
Below: *Side views of the 1980 Z28, showing the striking decals.*

The 5-liter Z28 engine was only now available with automatic three-speed, otherwise it had to be the 165-hp 5-liter four-speed manual.

All rear axle ratios were reduced, the 3.8-liter V6 was now standard on base cars and it was rated at 110 hp. Otherwise there was little to make a noise about apart from halogen headlamps and a wheel cover locking package.

1981 was a slow year, to some it was a drag and people were looking forward to the redesign, scheduled for 1982. *Car and Driver* got in on the "wonder-what" circuit by printing a story illustrated with spy photos of a mysterious new four-wheeled object speeding along on the GM proving ground in Michigan. There were some pretty accurate predictions (leaked?) of what the new design would be like, and they predicted "basic, duded-up Berlinetta and a hot-dog Z28."

In fact a total redesign was about to be unveiled.

Right: *A racing version of the 1981 Camaro, with* (below) *the 1981 Z28.*

The Z28 of 1982, the first year of the third generation of Camaros.

THE YEAR 1982

*T*he story of the 1982 Camaro continued to unfold. It began a long time before the long-awaited 1982 launch. The car body until then had evolved organically, growing, getting stronger and better. And the engineering had ridden all the legal and economic storms of the 1970s. It was time for a new design. But how do you replace a classic?

You don't. You design a car that is right up-to-date in style and engineering concepts, but you make damn sure that it's still recognizably from the same family. It's a difficult thing to do and cannot, however hard it tries, be done by a committee.

A lot of designs and a lot of clays were created in the years before, and all the new information from how the Camaro performed in reality was fed back into the system, as were the lessons learned from the new regulations, which spawned a whole new set of engineering problems and solutions.

The objective was a smaller car, lighter, neater, shorter but one that kept to the heritage "look" of Camaro. They were bending new materials to new shapes. There was also a big discussion going on about the placement of the engine drivetrain. Somewhere along the line the concept of front-wheel drive was taken seriously as it was one way to fuel efficiency. Sliding doors with fixed glass were considered, hidden headlamps, short dash-to-axle proportions. All of them seemed to feature low and ultralow fronts, picking up the fact that the soft nose bumper had created a low point at its very front. Single pane sideglass was another visually stunning feature.

The design went on over many years until in 1978 an assistant of Bill Porter's named Roger Hughet turned in a single drawing. Everyone knew that was it. They did renderings and then a model that convinced them all that here was the 1982 Camaro.

Hughet's Camaro was a wedge shape with fender lines that flowed back magically to a perky wedge-shaped rear which was complemented by a fiddle-back shaped backlight.

It was this reverse bend backlight that for many designers set the mood of the new car, and it was to prove devilishly difficult to actually produce – no one had ever made a bit of glass that shape and size before and at the right cost. The designers also decided seriously to go for a 63 degree windshield, challenging a GM house rule about the angle of front glass.

All along they had the added pressure of having to conform in certain common parts with Pontiac, with whom they fought in a most unfraternal way and won. They had battles over wheel opening shapes, rear quarters, compromising all the way and still fighting to retain their design.

Engineering staff declared they couldn't get those head-lamps as low as the designers wanted in order to get a "sneaky" look. Glass people said "no way" to the double bend, Fisher-Body said "no way" to the proposed rear glass support flange. The deadline for production was approaching and lots had to be done. For example, there was no space for the spare tire.

But all these problems and more were overcome. The interior had to work with all the new shapes around the inner space; that meant redesigning instrumentation and placing to eliminate possible reflection from the flatter windshield. Redesigning the display was an epic story in its own right. Another thing the designers were determined on was to give the Camaro fully adjustable seats. They came up with three levels of sophistication (and cost), the best of these being a super seat for the driver, available in the Z28.

Left: *Head of the advanced design studio – Bill Porter.*
Right: *Lloyd Reuss and (far right) Tom Zimmer were, respectively, Chevrolet chief engineer and Camaro chief engineer in the development period leading to 1982.*
Below: *A cutaway drawing of the new 1982 generation of Camaros which highlights the significant design and engineering innovations.*

1 Integrated front and rear bumpers using honeycomb energy management system.
2 Low hood line with quad rectangular headlamps.
3 Front disc brakes with power assist.
4 Responsive modified MacPherson-strut front suspension.
5 Stiff shock-absorbing strut tower.
6 Electronic control module accurately controls engine air/fuel ratios.
7 Fluidic windshield washers.
8 Hidden windshield wipers.
9 Powertrain offerings include 4-speed manual and optional 3-speed automatic transmissions.
10 Raked-back 62° windshield.
11 Low-drag mirrors.
12 Side window defoggers.
13 Flush-mounted aerodynamic windshield.
14 Hip-high integrated console.
15 Fully reclining seats with lateral restraint.
16 Comfortable 3-point restraint system.
17 Torque arm rear suspension.
18 Fold-down rear seat.
19 Sculptured glass liftback leads to 11.4 cu ft storage area.

Engineeringwise the car was designed with fuel economy in mind, and on-board computers became essential. And all the time it had to be smaller and shorter. The body frame was designed to be integral, or unit body, and this meant a total rethink on structure, which necessarily had to be more complex.

Suspension was stiffened up using a variant on the McPherson strut system. Independent suspension was considered but ruled out on grounds of tooling costs.

The final result was that rear axle assemblies covered the range of five ratios from 2.73:1 to 3.42:1. Brakes were disc front and drum rear. The master cylinder of aluminum had a plastic reservoir and easily checkable see-through window, the vacuum power booster was standard, and rear disc brakes optional.

The base 1982 Camaro had 14 × 6 wheels in body color while the Berlinetta had 14 × 7 cast aluminum wheels in gold, and the Z28's 14 × 7 had steel rally wheel in silver, charcoal, or gold.

A new engine option was the dual TBI, throttle-body injection 5-liter. The 2.5-liter also had TBI and the 2.8-liter V6 had a regular varajet carb. Other engines were the 5-liter 4 bbl V8 and the 5-liter dual TBI mentioned above, which was the standard for the Z28. Any of these power units could take the three-speed auto transmission with console shifter and converter clutch lock-up in third. The four-cylinder and V6 had a standard four-speed light duty Muncie manual and the TBI and V8 had a heavy duty Borg Warner.

1982 Camaros had a new exhaust system a transverse rear muffler with integral tailpipe led off from a catalytic converter, each muffler tuner in dimensions to each engine. The Z28 had dual exhausts with twin transverse resonators to produce a mellow voice beloved of drivers. The soft nose bumpers were body color and formed of urethane covered honeycomb "enersorbers" mounted on rigid impact bars; below it on the Z28 was the lower, mean-looking airdam.

The increased glass gave better visibility, and the seating was roomier even though the car was shorter (it lost out on storage space but people required more comfort than valises).

Dimensions were: length 184 inches (467 cm), wheelbase 101 inches (256.5 cm), tread widths 59.3 inches (150.6 cm), and cargo volume was 11.7 cu feet (0.331 cu m). The option list included T roofs, power windows and locks, electrically controlled outside mirrors, defoggers, washers and wipers, air conditioning, cruise control, rally wheels, power antenna, and a whole selection of audio gear.

The Camaro had in many senses grown up to be a responsible adult car, aware of safety, emission and damageability, environmentally friendly and yet exciting looking, and with a great deal of performance. And it was up to date, good looking and performance-orientated with good handling characteristics.

For many years now it had been the driver's friend, living up to its name. In 1982 a friendly future lay ahead.

Left: A 1982 Berlinetta, with the optional removable roof panels.
Below: The powerful, graceful lines of the 1982 Z28 are very clear in these views.

Above: For the third time in its history the Camaro was chosen, in 1982, to be the Indianapolis 500 pace car.

Previous pages: *The IROC-Z Convertible of 1987, which was available as an optional conversion.*

Below: *A simple cutaway drawing of the 1983 Camaro.*

Right: *The important selling features of the 1983 Z28.*

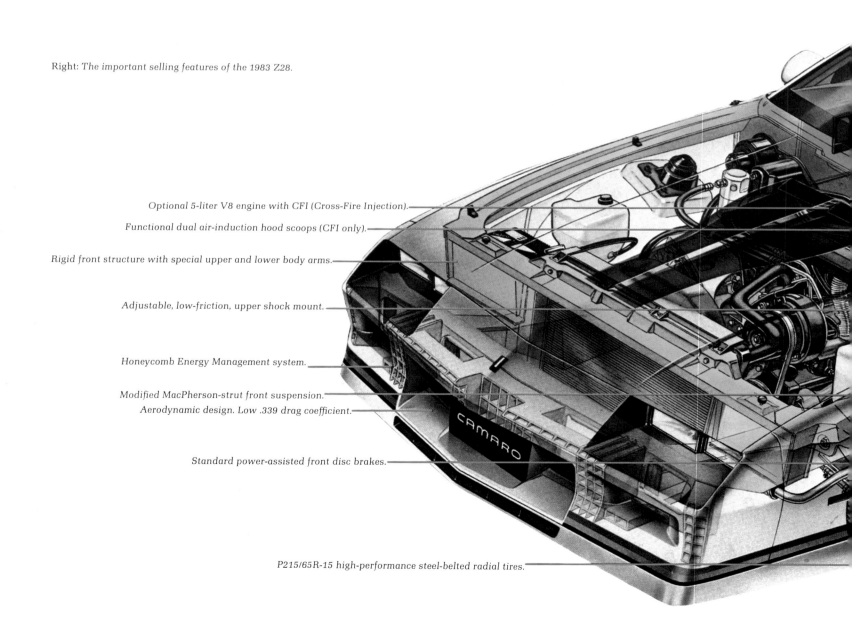

Optional 5-liter V8 engine with CFI (Cross-Fire Injection).

Functional dual air-induction hood scoops (CFI only).

Rigid front structure with special upper and lower body arms.

Adjustable, low-friction, upper shock mount.

Honeycomb Energy Management system.

Modified MacPherson-strut front suspension.

Aerodynamic design. Low .339 drag coefficient.

Standard power-assisted front disc brakes.

P215/65R-15 high-performance steel-belted radial tires.

For 1983 the big news was the introduction of two new economical transmissions—a five-speed manual (standard on the Z28 and the Berlinetta) and an option on the Sport Coupé. A four-speed automatic was optional on all three models.

Ratios in the five-speed manual varied according to what engine it was teamed with. For Camaros equipped with the 2.8 V6 the ratios were 3.5, 2.14, 1.36, 1.00 and 0.78. With the 5-liter V8 equipped with the four-barrel carburetor they were 2.95, 1.94, 1.34, 1.00 and 0.73. The 2.5-liter four-cylinder had the same as the V6 except that the fifth gear was 0.73 instead of 0.78.

The standard engine for the SC model remained the 2.5-liter four with electronic fuel injection, and a manual four-speed was standard. The 2.8-liter V6 with a two-barrel carb was an option for Sport Coupé models. Standard engine in the Berlinetta was the 2.8-liter V6 with the 5-speed manual gearbox.

Standard engine in the Z28 was the 5-liter V8 and four-barrel carb. An option was the 5-liter V8 with cross-fire fuel injection. Transmission was the five-speed manual gearbox and the four-speed automatic as an option. This unit had a converter clutch lock-up in second, third and fourth gears for maximum economy, with fourth acting as an overdrive giving quiet, restful high-speed cruising.

There were new exterior paint and interior trim colors for 1983, with the Z28 especially nicely fitted out in tri-tone colors. The Z28 also carried an even better stereo system. It came as no great shock to read in *Motor Trend* magazine at the end of 1983 that the Z28 was selected as "The Car of the Year"; it was also chosen as the Indianapolis 500 pace car and 6,360 commemorative examples were built.

The twin Camaro plants at Norwood, Ohio, and Van Nuys, California, continued to produce America's favorite 2 + 2 automobile.

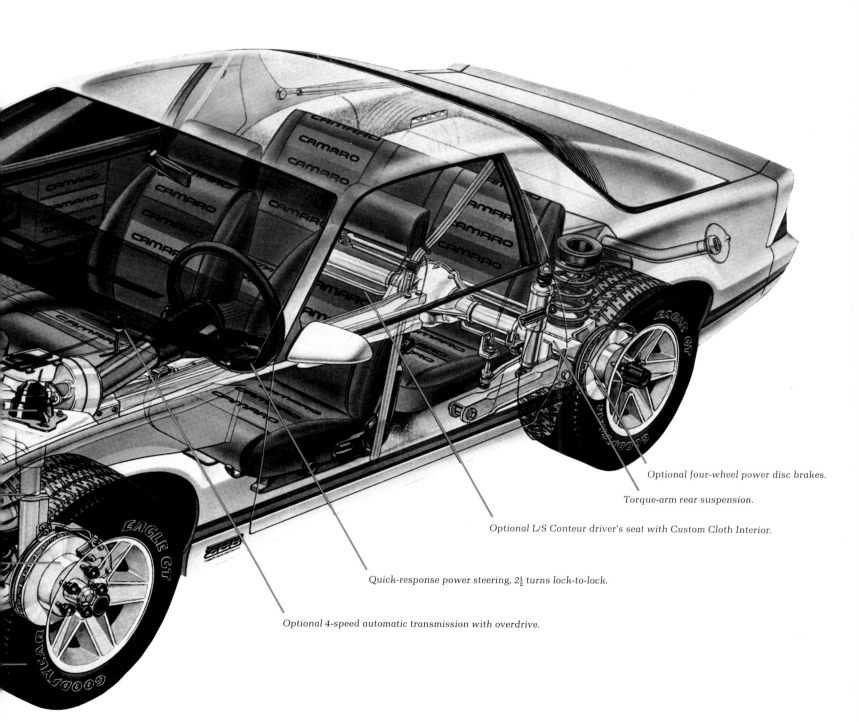

Optional four-wheel power disc brakes.

Torque-arm rear suspension.

Optional L/S Conteur driver's seat with Custom Cloth Interior.

Quick-response power steering, 2½ turns lock-to-lock.

Optional 4-speed automatic transmission with overdrive.

Right and below: *For the 1983 Z28 Sport Coupé a special HO (High Output) engine was available, at no extra cost, as well as the Cross-Fire Injection one.*

he three-model range continued into 1984, riding on the crest of a sales boom, but there was a cloud on the high performance 2 + 2 automobile horizon: the Japanese were equipping themselves for the challenge. Chevrolet expended great efforts to retain their hold on this very American segment of the market.

The performance of the Z28 was enough to keep old customers happy, and to make converts of new ones. Fitted with the L69 High Output 5-liter V8, rated at a modest 190 bhp at 5800 rpm with 240 lb/ft of torque at 3200 rpm, the Z28 took 19 seconds to cover the 0-100 mph dash, and an excellent 7.2 seconds for the benchmark 0-60 mph. Brake performance was equally good, especially with the optional four-wheel disc brakes fitted; the 100 mph to standstill needed 374 feet, in fact the Z28 was timed over the 0-100-0 acceleration and back to stop in 23.8 seconds.

In the land of the ridiculous 55 mph national speed limit, it is interesting to note that whilst Camaro literature features acceleration times, at no place does it even mention maximum speed!

The Berlinetta was highlighted in the brochure as an example of "Elegant Performance" and as one that makes any journey of more importance than if attempted in another make of 2 + 2. In truth there is no denying the fact that it was an auto that delivered that special brand of American muscle in a fine value-for-money package. This writer could find only two small details in the Berlinetta that he did not agree with – the digital

Below and right: Views of the 1984 Z28, which was chosen by Car and Driver *as the best handling car manufactured in the United States.*

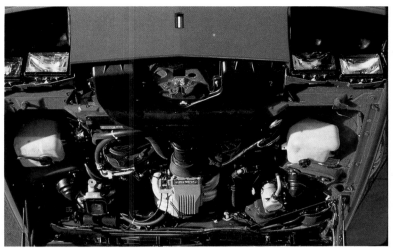

speedometer and the vertical strip rev-counter. Both in use were difficult to read quickly. The rest of the instrumentation was clear and easy to use. Much appreciated in hot California was the electronically controlled air conditioning system and the fine GM-Delco stereo radio/cassette unit. The LC1 V6 engine was smooth, producing a reasonable amount of power, but for real get-up-and-go the optional LG4 5-liter V8 was the way to go, especially with the four-speed auto transmission.

The Z28 was further reinforced as THE performance car in the Camaro range. With its High Output V8 engine, it shaved two seconds off the other two Camaros' times for the 0-60 mph and quarter-mile dashes. Code numbered L69, the HO engine featured a higher lift camshaft, and an improved ignition together with better intake and exhaust systems. Not even the wide-mouth catalytic converter could dampen down the real go of this car. Only the rather small fuel tank, at 16.2 gallons, prevented the Z28 from becoming the ultimate trans-continental personal express.

The 1984 Berlinetta, which justifiably received special treatment in General Motors' publicity for that year. It combined grand touring comfort with refined instrumentation and over-all elegance.

The hot news for the 1985 model year at Chevrolet was the introduction of the IROC-Z28. Based on the competing cars in the International Race of Champions series, the new Camaro was set to be a sure-fire winner on the roads and in the showrooms of the USA.

The LB9 V8 engine featured Tuned-Port Injection to produce 215 bhp and 275 lb/ft of torque. It was a marvelous engine, not at all peaky or difficult to drive in heavy traffic conditions. The IROC-Z28 had as standard the excellent five-speed transmission, higher ratio power steering at $2\frac{1}{2}$ turns from lock to lock, and P245/50VR-16 tires on beautiful alloy road wheels. The whole automobile sat lower than any previous Camaro, which gave it improved handling and roadholding. The rear suspension carried gas-filled Delco/Bilstein shock absorbers and the standard power-assisted all-ventilated disc brakes made stopping as easy as the going.

The Berlinetta and Sport Coupé continued much the same as in 1984 with a few improvements and changes to interior trim and colors. The cars were still selling well, and there appeared to be no good reason to make changes unnecessarily. The show stayed on the road for 1985.

Below: *A line-up of the IROC-Z – new in 1985 and widely acclaimed – and the Z28.*
Right: *The new 2.8 MFI (Multi-port Fuel Injection) V6 engine was standard for the Berlinetta in 1985.*
Far right: *The rear aspect of the Z28.*

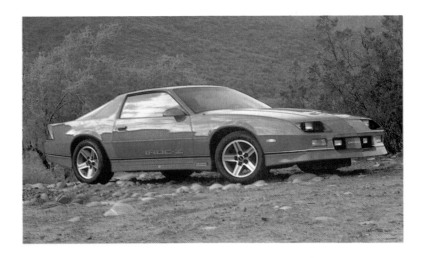

Careful perusal of the 1986 Camaro brochure revealed several interesting figures in the official performance tables. Compared to the 1984 Z28 with the HO engine, the 1986 car with Tuned-Port Injection, giving the same horse-power (190 bhp) but 45 more lb/ft of torque, was slower by 0.2 seconds in acceleration for the 0-60 mph run, 2.4 seconds slower for the 0-100 mph, stopped in five feet less distance for the 60 mph to stop area, and lost out by .05g in the lateral acceleration measurement. It was obvious that GM were slowing the Camaros down, but to balance this the car was easier to drive faster, and safer than the 1984 model. It was nearly 100 lb heavier, but fuel consumption was virtually the same. Very puzzling.

With the Sport Coupé the Chevrolet development department were given the task of making it more like the Z28 without the compromises entailed in that all-performance machine. The first thing they did was to replace the standard wheels and tires with P205/70R-14 radials mounted on rally-style wheels. There was for all Camaros a new base coat/clear coat finish, together with twin door-mounted rear view mirrors.

The suspension gained new gas shock absorbers, and was carefully retuned to work with the new tires and wheels. A 2.8-liter V6 with multi-port injection was added, together with a five-speed gearbox and a lower ratio rear axle.

The result was yet another tremendous value-for-money performance car called Camaro. It sold like hot cakes.

New all-cloth interiors were introduced for the Sport Coupé, Z28 and IROC-Z28 models. The Comfortilt steering wheel and the new six-way adjustable power-operated driver's seat further increased the already good cabin environment. Glass removable T-tops were carried over from the 1985 option range and proved to be very popular on the Z28 in particular.

Facing page: Three of the 1986 models – the IROC-Z, Z28 and Sport Coupé.
Below: In 1986, the Berlinetta was phased out.

Above: The IROC-Z package increased in popularity in 1986, selling twice as many as in 1985.

hevrolet have always been a performance-orientated division of General Motors Corporation and for very many years they have operated a racing budget of ten million and more dollars. The Chaparral racing car was a recipient of Chevrolet's money and, more importantly, Chevrolet's skills for its total competition life. When it comes to making solid, reliable high-performance cars, they know as much (and more) than any other major automobile maker in the world. 1987 provides a glimpse of their capability. A new engine came into the Camaro range. The L98 arrived with a capacity of 5.7 liters in its V8 configuration. Tuned-Port Injection produced 225 bhp at 4400 rpm with a muscular 330 lb/ft of torque at a very usable 2800 rpm. Overall weight of the model went up by 131 lb, but fuel consumption remained very much the same as in the lesser engine from the previous year. Maybe the roller-hydraulic valve lifters delivered their promised three percent fuel economy benefit?

Acceleration was cut to 6.3 seconds for the 0-60 mph sprint, and the quarter-mile dash took only 14.5 seconds. Lateral acceleration was up to .88g measured on the skid-pad, helped by the impressive P245/50VR-16 Goodyear Eagle GT radial tires.

New optional leather seats and an optional Delco/Bose stereo system provided a high quality driving environment to the IROC-Z's lucky owner. No wonder 25 percent of all Camaros ordered were to the IROC-Z specification!

For 1987 the Berlinetta name was dropped and the base model LT was introduced. Much the same as the Berlinetta, the LT featured a "Boulevard Ride" suspension package, thus losing the sharpness of handling of the other Camaros but appealing to those buyers who want the Camaro looks and charisma, with a softer, more resilient ride. A much quieter exhaust system further emphasized this aspect of the model.

Among the vast array of options for the Camaro, the rear window louvers continued from the previous year's offerings. Electronic cruise control and an automatic day/night mirror gave further evidence of Chevrolet's insistence on giving the driver the best of driving aids.

Below: *The 1987 Camaro Z28.*
Right: *In 1987 an LT option was offered for the Sport Coupé as a grand touring alternative to the phased-out Berlinetta.*

Above: *The 1987 IROC-Z with (left) the 5-liter Tuned Port Injection engine which was an option.*

Below: *Also available was the Sport Coupé, "without any tinsel" said the brochure.*

Facing page: *Convertible versions of Camaros became possible in 1987, the first since 1969. These views are of the IROC-Z.*

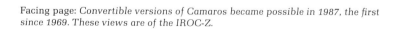

Only two versions of the Camaro were available in the 1988 model year – the Sport Coupé and the IROC-Z models. A convertible version was included for both cars. There were four engine options: the LB8 V6 injected engine producing 135 bhp at 4000 rpm and an excellent 160 lb/ft of torque at 3900 rpm; the LO3 injected V8 5-liter engine had 170 bhp at 4000 rpm and a remarkable 255 lb/ft of torque at 2400 rpm; the LB9 Tuned-Port Injection V8 5-liter made 220 bhp at 4400 rpm (manual transmission), 195 bhp (automatic) and 290 lb/ft of torque at 3200 rpm (manual) and 295 lb/ft of torque at 2800 rpm (automatic); and the L98 5.7-liter V8 gained a little more HP up to 230 bhp at 4400 rpm and 330 lb/ft of torque at 3200 rpm.

The coupé version of the IROC-Z remained much as the previous year's car, but the convertible version was a sensation. Daniel Charles Ross of *Motor Trend* magazine suggested that on the street it is simply impossible to ignore the IROC-Z and in this writer's experience this is an understatement. It is a head-turner. If you have a retiring nature it could almost be an embarrassment to drive in the convertible. Seating four adults in comfort, with an enclosed lockable trunk, it is the perfect sunshine performance car, bar none. Interiors of both Camaro models were improved even further with a leather trimmed interior as the high spot.

From its earliest days the Camaro has given its buyer the most value for money in a performance car. Year by year Chevrolet have updated the model to retain old customers, attract new buyers and fight off the opposition. In recent years GM have slipped behind the Ford Motor Company in over-all sales figures. Considerable confusion within the management structure has exacerbated this situation with the result that many new models have been developed but not put into production, much market goodwill has been lost to other car makers, and above all else the General have lost time and their touch with the customer. However, through all these recent difficulties Chevrolet have kept faith with the Camaro. For almost 25 years they have shown that they know what the customer wants and they have been seen to succeed – and long may it be so.

Below: The 1988½ RS model, which had been introduced in 1987 exclusively in California, was a sporty Camaro with many IROC features.

Facing page: The 1988 IROC-Z in its Convertible and Coupé versions.

Following pages, top: The Camaro Sport Coupé of 1988.
Below: The Convertible and Sport Coupé versions of the 1988 IROC-Z.

The Camaro RS of 1989.

1989

here was in fact to be virtually no change in 1989. Instead, the successful innovations of 1988 were consolidated. In particular the IROC-Z Convertible continued to hold the admiring attention of the buying public and the usually hard-to-please motoring press. It possessed an overall balance between its distinctive visual appeal and its outstanding engineering virtues, with comfort and roominess as strong supporting features – coupled of course to an attractive price tag. It was a winning combination.

The 1989 Camaro range as a whole, limited though it was numerically, continued to possess great sales appeal and the public remained pleased. As a European dealer remarked approvingly, the Camaro is still a classic American car, with its general "feel," its analog instrumentation layout, and the 5-liter engine giving a unique distinction in road handling and power.

Meanwhile the show went on, but with Chevrolet using 1989 as a year of planning and development in preparation for the 1990's and for the evolutionary advance of the Camaro, with

value for money for the buyer as still the dominant aim and, indeed, very real achievement. Great things were in store for the future.

Available in Coupé and Convertible versions, the 1989 RS had a 2.8-liter V6 multi-port engine, with a number of "sporty" features including an IROC-Z appearance. Its Convertible (below) was just as attractive.

The 1989 IROC-Z was an outstanding all-rounder, and especially in its Convertible version.

INTO THE 1990'S

The IROC-Z, still superb in 1990.

eneral Motors are a conservative organization. "Evolution not Revolution" is their motto, and they will hold fast to this as they enter the last decade of the twentieth century. Despite many efforts to change it, the Camaro of the 1990's will stay true to the General Motors' line. This one consideration must never be forgotten when trying to forecast the next decade's Camaro models. Commercial and financial risks are so great, that mistakes could have dire consequences for company, management and workers alike, should too great a change of model design be made.

Consider the words of James Perkins, Chevrolet general manager: "The future Camaro will not stray far from the current concept. It will stay a rear-wheel drive vehicle, with many of the current powerstrains, but with improved suspension and body structure." These may appear overly cautious words, but with over five million satisfied buyers of the F-body model and the established goodwill that the car has earned, it is only to be expected that proposed changes should be considered most carefully.

It makes good sense to carry over features and components that retain the special qualities of the Camaro and can fight off the opposition, such as the V-6/V-8 engines. To effect changes in the design of the automobile for the sake of mere styling change is no longer a valid reason and changes must improve the vehicle, both dynamically and cosmetically.

Added pressure on the Camaro market from other makers, foreign and domestic, will force General Motors to follow this evolutionary line. Strong hints of what is in store for Camaro buyers in the next ten years could be seen at the January 1989 Los Angeles Show. On display was the "Concept Camaro IROC-Z". This auto has a wheel base of 104 inches (2.6 m), and an overall length of 186 inches. The chassis design highlights an all-independent suspension set-up, four-wheel disc brakes, and 17-inch Goodyear tires. The engine is a DOHC V-6, but there

Above: *The 1990 Camaro RS.*
Below: *The 5-liter V8 engine with EFI used in the RS and IROC-Z.*
Above right: *The Camaro shape of things to come in the 1990's.*

were no details of its capacity, or its horse-power. The Concept Camaro's body will be made of steel, which is slightly at odds with GM's very great interest in non-metallic bodywork, especially as they have already gone into production of the Chevrolet Lumina All-purpose Vehicle which uses panels in "New, High-Strength, Reinforced, Advanced Composite Material." Light in weight, non-rusting, and very easily replaced should they be damaged, these body panels would appear to be perfect for the Camaro, but as yet there is no word from GM that they will use them. Maybe this is an area in which their conservatism is misplaced?

From sneaked photographs of development Camaros it would appear that the 1990's Camaro will reflect strong European GM influences. The "Soft Line Look" is obviously in, out has gone the hard-edged masculine line of recent models and the Opel influence is here. Front-wheel drive was explored with the GM-80 experimental models, but this was considered to be too radical, and was quietly put to one side. Maybe later, towards the end of the century, this will be revived?

For the lovers of hi-tech automotive design and innovation some of the details that have come out regarding this GM-80 vehicle have been enough to make the mouth water. Just consider the power unit, a DOHC V6 with a 4 valves per cylinder configuration, coupled to an electronic four-speed automatic transaxle! A lightweight, hyper-aerodynamic, composite paneled body fitted with this marvelous power unit sounds just like the Camaro of the future – and for the rest of the world, not just North America. Built at the rate that General Motors are capable of, it could rule the automotive world for years to come.

But it is not to be. The traditionalists within the GM organization could not bring themselves to approve the GM-80 design, and like so many previous GM prototypes the GM-80 has been buried. Cost cutting was the official reason given, but basically it was killed off because there are some in GM who are out of touch with the buying public, and are simply too frightened to take too big a step into the future!

What can the Camaro-buyer of the early 1990's expect? For sure some of the GM-80 prototype details *will* appear in the model code-named CF4, or fourth-generation Camaro/Firebird. First, the car will be shorter by as much as a foot and several hundred pounds lighter. It will feature a new steel space frame chassis, similar to the old Pontiac Fiero model. It could also carry both steel and composite body panels. This later feature of the Camaro seems to indicate that body styling changes could come along more frequently than in the recent past, because composite material, is cheaper, faster, and easier to alter than steel. Composite material for bodywork will also allow General Motors divisional design studios to make each marque more individual within the GM Corporation. In other words, a Chevy will look nothing like a Pontiac, or Oldsmobile, and this can only be to the good!

Between 1990 and 1993 the Camaro is set to have an all-independent rear suspension featuring a transverse fiber-glass single leaf spring, and controlled by multi-links. There will be a number of suspension options available, peaking with the option of 17-inch, Z-rated, Goodyear Gatorbacks high-performance tires.

Engines will not be so predictable, depending as they will on upcoming Federal standards. The expected new fuel economy regulations could well drive out the present V6/V8 power-plants, and accelerate the introduction of a small displacement 4-liter V8 unit. This engine type might well be offered with both SOHC and DOHC configurations, with power outputs ranging from 225 bhp to 275 bhp. There is also a DOHC V6 with 24 valves of 3.4-liter capacity waiting in the wings. Immediate usable engine options cover the 2.3-liter Quad-4, and the turbo 3.1-liter, plus the 4.3-liter V6 and 5-liter V8 engines.

Transmissions include the present Chev/Getrag five-speed gearbox, and the four-speed automatic, with the possibility of the Borg-Warner six-speed unit being utilized. Rumors get steadily stronger by the day concerning a new electronic, hi-efficiency four-speed auto-box coming through for the mid-1990's.

On the down side it is clear that the Camaro of the 1990's will have less power and performance than its makers would have liked to deliver. For instance, it was hoped to offer 300 bhp and a 5–6 seconds time for the 0–60 mph in their top of the line models, but it was not to be. Viewing the Camaro positively into the near future, it would appear that the line from the 1967 originals can still be traced through to the present cars; they will go better, stop better, and handle better than previous models. Camaros will continue to be wonderful value-for-money performance automobiles; in other words, they will not have priced themselves out of the pockets of entry-level enthusiasts.

Index

Page numbers in *italic* figures refer
to illustrations in the text.

Acknowledgments

The Publishers acknowledge with thanks the help of General Motors Corporation, Chevrolet Division, for providing information, photographs and illustrations, and the following for supplying photographs from their libraries:

Ludvigsen Associates Ltd: pp. 36–7, 38 (above and below), 39, 82 (above), and 104 (below).

Mr John McGovren: title page (right), pp. 83 and 85 (inset).

Mr Andy Willsheer: title page (left), 6–7, 30–1, 32, 34 (below), 35 (above and below), 40 (below), 41 (below), 44–5, 46–7, 48–9, 50–1, 52 (below), 56 (above), 57 (above), 58–9, 60–1, 65 (above and below), 66–7, 68–9, 70 (below), 71 (below), 73, 76 (above), 77 (above and below), 78–9, 80 (below), 81 (below), 82 (below, right), 84, 85 (below), 86–7, 90, 91, 94 (above), 99 (above), 100–1, 105 (above), 108 (above and below), 109, 110, 112, 112–3 and 116 (above).